A Pilgrim's Testament

THE MEMOIRS OF SAINT IGNATIUS OF LOYOLA

EDITED BY

Barton T. Geger, S.J.

Cover: *Ignatius at Manresa* by Albert Chevalier-Tayler (1908)
© 2011/12 Jesuit Institute London

Library of Congress Control Number: 2020941370

ISBN: 978-1-947617-05-6

Copyright 2020 by the Jesuit Conference, Inc., United States.

Institute of Jesuit Sources
at the Institute for Advanced Jesuit Studies
Boston College
140 Commonwealth Avenue | Chestnut Hill, MA 02467 | USA

email: iajs@bc.edu
http://jesuitsources.bc.edu

Fees are subject to change

**INSTITUTE FOR
ADVANCED JESUIT STUDIES**
BOSTON COLLEGE

A Pilgrim's Testament
The Memoirs of Saint Ignatius of Loyola

Revised Edition

Edited by Barton T. Geger, S.J.

Contents

Preface

This second edition of *A Pilgrim's Testament* retains the translation of the first edition (1983, reprinted 1995 and 2006) by the late Fr. Parmananda R. Divarkar (1922–2000) of the Society of Jesus. Variants of this translation appeared in *Ignatius of Loyola: Spiritual Exercises and Selected Works*, ed. George E. Ganss, S.J., Classics of Western Christianity Series (New York: Paulist Press, 1991); *Ablaze with God: A Reading of the Memoirs of Ignatius of Loyola* (Anand, India: Gujarat Sahitya Prakash, 1990); and *Testament and Testimony: The Memoirs of Ignatius of Loyola* (Anand, India: Gujarat Sahitya Prakash, 1994).

I lightly revised Fr. Divarkar's translation for clarity and style. Excessive pronouns often rendered the identities of protagonists unclear, so I replaced some with their proper nouns, including additional appearances of "the pilgrim." I changed some vocabulary to illuminate subtleties in the text that would otherwise go unnoticed.

I use endnotes instead of footnotes so that readers will not be distracted from the story. Hopefully, the more substantial notes that this makes possible will compensate for the inconvenience.

I am grateful to my colleagues at the Institute for Advanced Jesuit Studies (IAJS) for their assistance with this project. I also thank Fr. Milton T. Walsh, Dr. Catherine Mooney, Dr. Joseph DeFeo, and Jesuit companions Fr. Paul Harmon, Fr. Kenneth Hughes, Fr. André Brouillette, Fr. Thomas Cwik, and Fr. James Carr. I am grateful to Ms. Rebecca Hammock of IAJS for her patient correction of cross-references.

—BTG

Introduction

For information about the abbreviations used in the introduction and throughout the book, see appendix 3.

St. Ignatius of Loyola (*c.*1491–1556) was a Spanish nobleman who had a spiritual conversion when he was thirty years old. Since his youth, he had been a proud Catholic Christian, even if his behavior was not always exemplary in that regard. After his conversion, he radically re-appropriated his old faith. He fell in love with God in a new way, and so experienced a sense of peace, and a sense of meaning, that he had not known before. He dedicated the rest of his life to helping other people experience a similar transformation in their own lives.

Ignatius did two things for which he is famous. First, he wrote a little book called *The Spiritual Exercises*, which is a manual of sorts to guide people through a thirty-day silent retreat. In the 1,500 years of church history before him, many Christians had written books on how to pray, but Ignatius was one of the first to write a book on how to make a retreat. Since then, it has become a classic of Christian literature.

The second thing that Ignatius did, after he became a Catholic priest, was to create a fraternity of priests and lay brothers called the Society of Jesus, or the Jesuits for short. He did this with nine other priests, two of whom were St. Francis Xavier (1506–52) and St. Peter Faber (1506–46). Ignatius wanted Jesuits to be highly trained and mobile, ready to go at a moment's notice to wherever the needs of the church were greatest. This was new in the history of the church. No other group of Catholic priests or laypeople had ever dedicated itself so specifically to mobility and adaptability.

The early Jesuits elected Ignatius their first leader, or "superior general." Here, "general" does not mean military general. It means a superior with the highest authority, in the same sense that the attorney general and surgeon general of the United States are the highest

1

authorities in its legal and medical fields. Jesuits make a vow of obedience, so that their superior general can mission them to wherever the church needs them. Ignatius held this office for the last sixteen years of his life. During that time, he saw the Society of Jesus grow from ten men to almost a thousand. Today, there are about sixteen thousand Jesuits around the world.

A Pilgrim's Testament is the story of pivotal events in Ignatius's life, told mostly in his own words. But why should anyone want to read it today?

For starters, one could make a good argument that, in the last five centuries, the Society of Jesus has been one of the most influential groups in the history of Western culture, and perhaps even the world. It has certainly been one of the most controversial. For that reason, Jesuit history is a subject that both Catholic and secular scholars have been researching heavily since the late twentieth century. They want to understand the *way of proceeding*—as Jesuits like to call it—of this body of men: the principles of Jesuit education, or the ways that Jesuit missionaries engaged non-Christian cultures, or the advice that Jesuit mystics and spiritual writers gave people about prayer and their relationships with God. Today, many people believe that this Jesuit way of proceeding still has much relevance: it has deeply influenced, for example, Pope Francis's (1936–, r.2013–) manner of leading the Catholic Church. And so, in order to understand it better, one needs to know something about the man who was largely responsible for it.

A second reason to care about *A Pilgrim's Testament* is that readers will find Ignatius struggling with many of the same questions and tensions that Christians face every day: Why should I belong to the church, if I can follow God in my own way? What should I do with my life? How do I fight this temptation? How do I know when God is trying to tell me something? Is it ever acceptable to say "no" to good people who ask for my help?

In *A Pilgrim's Testament*, Ignatius does not articulate these questions in so many words. But it is fair to say that most of the stories he shares with readers do revolve around those themes. Usually, he does not find the answers right away. He makes mistakes, and he changes his mind about things. And he continues to live with certain tensions.

Readers might not agree with all of Ignatius's emphases or choices. That is not necessarily a bad thing. One reason Catholic Christians love the communion of saints is that it reminds people that there is more than one way to be holy. To tell the truth, even some of the first Jesuits—holy men in their own right—were not entirely comfortable with some of Ignatius's emphases and choices (see, e.g., Ch. 3, no. 18). But if this book helps readers identify the spiritual tensions in their own lives, or if it gives them tools to engage with the questions more deeply—and perhaps most importantly, if it gives them courage to believe that they too can serve God in real holiness—then the book will have served the purpose that Ignatius intended.

The Inspiration behind the *Testament*

The early Jesuits recognized that Ignatius was a living saint. When he was superior general, they frequently asked him to tell stories about his youth, his conversion, and his adventures in the service of God. In fact, one of Ignatius's aides at the Jesuit headquarters in Rome—his name was Fr. Luís Gonçalves da Câmara (*c.*1519–75)—once remarked that he heard Ignatius tell the same stories "ten, fifteen, or more times," and always with great consistency (Eaglestone §99).

Finally, Jesuits asked Ignatius to put his story in writing. A book could inspire and guide readers for many years after he was gone. At first, he was extremely reluctant to do this. He had struggled with vanity his entire life, and he was afraid that he might have mixed motives. And even if his intention were pure, some people probably would conclude that he was being vain anyway. It might even scandalize them. For those reasons, whenever someone asked Ignatius about it, he essentially responded, "Maybe later."

Jesuits continued to pester Ignatius about it. After several years, he changed his mind. The reason—as two early Jesuits will relate in their forewords to this book—was that he began to recognize the truth of what they had been telling him, that his stories gave people consolation and strength in their own relationships with God. And if there was one thing that Ignatius knew for certain, it was that he wanted *helping souls*—as he liked to put it—to be the most import-ant consideration in his life. In other words, if he knew that a cer-tain course of action would help a greater number of people, then he should not let his fears about his own motives stop him, nor fears about how a lesser number of people will perceive him.

Ignatius chose Gonçalves to be the one to whom he told his story. The two men met four times between 1553 and 1555. Ignatius began with a detailed account of the sins of his youth, while Gonçalves listened carefully. Immediately after each session, Gonçalves made brief notes. Then, a few days or perhaps even a few weeks after each session, he retold Ignatius's stories to Jesuit scribes. They wrote down word-for-word what Gonçalves said. (But like all scribes, they occa-sionally wrote down the wrong words; e.g., see Ch. 3, no. 13.)

Gonçalves did not give the book a title. But another early Jesuit named Fr. Jerónimo Nadal (1507–1580) called it *Acta P. Ignatii* in Latin, which means *Acts of Our Father Ignatius*. Today, those who translate the book into English usually prefer to call it something else: the *Autobiography* of Ignatius, or *Story*, or *Memoirs*, or *Remi-niscences*. The translator of this present edition, Fr. Parmananda Divarkar, called it a *Testament*, and more specifically, *A Pilgrim's Tes-tament*. He borrowed that word from something Nadal wrote in his foreword, that other saints had left memoirs to their followers "by way of a testament" (*vice testamenti*).

An obvious question is whether Gonçalves changed anything that Ignatius had said to him. The idea that he could repeat Ignatius's words verbatim seems implausible, even if he really did have the remarkable memory that people said. But how different is it? Gonçalves might have changed only a few words or nuances. Or he might have gone further, by changing details, or re-arranging the order of the stories, or perhaps even adding or removing stories altogether.

The truth is complicated. For one thing, readers will not find Ignatius's name mentioned anywhere in the *Testament*. He is always *the pilgrim*, or simply *he*. It is difficult to imagine that Ignatius kept referring to himself in the third person for hours on end when dictating to Gonçalves. More likely, it was Gonçalves who added *the pilgrim* when dictating to the scribes. On the other hand, Ignatius probably asked him to do it. By replacing his name *Ignatius* with *the pilgrim*, readers might be more inclined to see themselves in the story, and it would reduce any impression that Ignatius was trying to glorify himself.

In thirteen places, scribes wrote Gonçalves's own comments in the margins of the manuscript. (These comments are included in the endnotes of this book.) But there are other places where the scribes inserted his comments directly into the text. One obvious example is in *Test.* §73. But there are other places where the language suddenly shifts from the third person to the first person, and these should probably be interpreted as Gonçalves's own comments (e.g., *Test.* §30, 41, 47, 54, 56, 59).

In *A Pilgrim's Testament*, readers will find many subtle references to the Bible, and to beloved, classic works of Christian literature like the *Imitation of Christ*. Moreover, some stories have been arranged in a certain way to make theological points. See, for example, *Test.* §28–30, where Ignatius stops telling his stories in chronological order, so that he can systematically present five different mystical experiences; or *Test.* §32–33, where he recounts three different close encounters with death that depict an evolution in his feelings about seeing God face-to-face. It seems highly unlikely that he could have kept all these details organized in his head while speaking to Gonçalves. So it seems that Gonçalves did some cutting-and-pasting.

But none of this means that *A Pilgrim's Testament* is fiction. Far from it. For one thing, if readers compare the book with other lives of Ignatius that were written by early Jesuits at about the same time (see appendix 2, 11–12), readers will find that they cover many of the same stories, in much the same language, and with most of the same details. Early Jesuits also referred to many of Ignatius's stories in their letters, and in their own memoirs. So readers can be confident that the *Testament* is an accurate record of what Ignatius said to Gonçalves, in all essential respects.

But for all these reasons, *A Pilgrim's Testament* is not really an autobiography in the modern sense, even if people often call it that. Ignatius made no pretense of trying to cover all the pivotal moments in his life. He does not refer to his momentous decisions to become a priest, to recruit men to join him, to create the Society of Jesus, and to make *the greater glory of God* the heart of the Jesuit mission. He says nothing about the vows that he and his companions made at the University of Paris in 1534, nor about the historic day that they offered their services to the pope in fulfilment of those vows.

Most likely, the reason for these omissions was that the superior general was preoccupied with other very serious matters, such as writing the *Constitutions*, answering hundreds of letters from around the world, missioning his fellow Jesuits, and protecting their lives and health. It is safe to say that he was distracted. It is also possible that he did not want to spend time dictating stories that early Jesuits already knew well. In *Test.* §98, for example, he ends his dictation abruptly by saying that Nadal could finish the rest.

But even if gaps exist in the story, Ignatius did emphasize certain ideas quite strongly. These are important for readers today, because they give a sense of at least some of the things that Ignatius wanted Jesuits and others to know about his values. Here are five such themes. Readers will be able to identify others.

1. The Catholic Tradition

That idea that Ignatius and/or Gonçalves changed the details of the stories, or rearranged the order of the stories, can trouble modern readers. Today, people usually want historians to be as accurate and objective as possible, and to describe events as they really happened, and in the right order.

In fact, this is a recent notion about how to write history. It goes back less than two hundred years. Before then, in ancient and medieval times, Christians took it for granted that people who wrote about the lives of saints (called *hagiographers*) changed the details in order to show how their heroes exemplified the lessons and patterns set by other saints.

This includes the four Gospels in the Bible. Matthew, Mark, Luke, and John told the historical truth about Jesus, but they also arranged the individual stories, and finessed the details, in order to emphasize certain themes that were important to them. Luke, for example, wanted to highlight the attention that Jesus gave to women, and so he re-arranged the stories so that Jesus was always helping a man and a woman at about the same time.

Following this pattern, Ignatius and Gonçalves often allude to famous stories of saintly heroes of the past, and to bits of wisdom about the spiritual life that Christians had been handing down for over a thousand years. If Ignatius gave readers the impression that he had discovered these ideas on his own, or that he was ignoring the wisdom of those who came before him, then he would be guilty of pride, or at least seem like it. In the *Spiritual Exercises*, he wrote that it would be like "building our nest in a house which belongs to Another," meaning that Christians attribute to themselves knowledge and gifts that they really got from God and from other people (§322).

Today, Western culture values the creation of new knowledge. Students who write dissertations, for example, are expected to make arguments that no one has made before. If they simply repeat what the experts say, they will be accused of laziness or plagiarism. But in medieval times—and still today, in some places around the world—people earned their doctorates when they could repeat and explain what everyone else had said. Saying something new was looked upon with suspicion. Consequently, when early Jesuits read the *Testament*, and they saw that their founder embodied so many aspects of the earlier tradition, they would have considered this proof that he was a spiritual master, not an argument against it.

If modern readers of *A Pilgrim's Testament* are unaware of its many allusions to the Catholic tradition, they can misinterpret certain stories, or give disproportionate weight to certain ideas. For example, as noted earlier, Ignatius makes frequent reference to the idea that he learned about God from his lived experience, as opposed to learning about God from books. Today, writers sometimes claim that Ignatius was one of the first saints in the church—if not *the* first saint—to emphasize this. That is far from true. Ironically, the theme of holy people learning from lived experience was a conventional theme in the history of Christian literature, starting as early as the Bible (see Ch. 3, no. 21).

Also, *learning from experience* can mean different things. It can mean that Ignatius learned something from scratch, entirely on his own, which is how people today often interpret what he says in the *Testament*. If that were true, then he would not need a tradition to guide him, nor the teachings of the church, nor the examples of the saints. But perhaps *learning from experience* meant that his lived experiences of God helped him to appropriate at a deeper level certain ideas that he already knew in a more abstract, theoretical way from the Bible and the earlier tradition. And in fact, Ignatius describes this very process in the *Spiritual Exercises* §2.

In the *Testament*, Ignatius uses many words that appear ordinary and unremarkable at first glance: words like *resolution, intention, patience, life, tears, sleep,* and *disgust*. In reality, all these were "buzzwords" in the Catholic spirituality of the sixteenth century. A thousand years before Ignatius, for example, a famous writer named St. John Cassian (*c*.360–*c*.435) had used the words *sleep* and *disgust* to describe the symptoms of a spiritual disease called *acedia*. Therefore, when early Jesuits were reading the *Testament*, and they saw these words in the story about Ignatius's scruples (*Test.* §25), they would have recognized a meaning to the story that eludes most readers today (see Ch. 3, no. 16).

The principal aim of this edition of *A Pilgrim's Testament* is to help readers appreciate how its stories and its spiritual wisdom are consistent with, reminiscent of, or inspired by, the Catholic tradition in the 1,500 years before Ignatius. In that sense, it differs from other editions that focus on names, dates, and historical details. In appendix 2 at the back of this book, readers will find a short list of some classic works that influenced Ignatius and Gonçalves. Each has its own abbreviation in the endnotes, so that readers can see points of contact between Ignatius and the tradition.

2. Service to Others

In the sixteenth century, many Catholics in Spain and Portugal believed that long hours of prayer, fasting, and solitude were necessary to grow in holiness. Some writers recommended as many as six or seven hours of prayer every day. These Catholics often believed that serving other people in spiritual and corporal works of mercy was risky, because it distracted them from their prayer, and it exposed them to the sinful temptations of the world around them.

At first, Ignatius seems to have shared this mentality. Shortly after his conversion, he spent eleven months in the town of Manresa, first living in a hospice among the sick, then in the homes of various new friends, such as the widow Inés Pascual (*c*.1468–1548) and her son Juan. He fasted and prayed for many hours daily. He rarely bathed, and he let his hair and fingernails grow unkempt, in order to fight his vanity.

At the same time, however, Ignatius noticed two things. First, the spiritual conversations he was having with townspeople were very effective for helping them grow in their own relationships with God. Second, some people were reluctant to talk to him, because he smelled bad and looked dangerous.

As a result, an unexpected question began to weigh on him. Which should take priority? Focusing on the fight with his own vanity? Or focusing on the spiritual care of others?

At some point during his stay in Manresa, Ignatius became convinced that the *care of souls*, as he liked to put it, should be the most important consideration in his life. Every decision that he made, great or small, should be based on that consideration. Years later, he told an early Jesuit named Diego Laínez (1512–65) that he believed that God would never fail to protect him, or to welcome him into heaven, provided that Ignatius kept his eyes fixed firmly on God and serving his people. After all, Ignatius reasoned, what human king, if he offered a great favor to a servant, and the servant refused it for the sake of being able to serve the king even more—what king in that situation would not feel obliged to protect the servant, and to grant him an even greater reward later? And if a human king does this for a servant whom he hardly knows, how much more will God reward those whom he loves infinitely, and who are entirely dedicated to his service? (*FontNarr.* 4:775; see also *SpirEx.* §91–100).

Ignatius had a mystical experience in Manresa that seems to have confirmed and strengthened his decision to serve others (*Test.* §30). God illuminated his mind about how God is intimately present in every person and place, at every moment. Even more, God is continually laboring, so to speak, to bring every human being closer to himself. This mystical illumination gave Ignatius increased optimism about the fruits to be gained by "working with God," and by casting the net widely.

Years later, Ignatius made the expression *for the greater glory of God* the unofficial motto of the Society of Jesus. This meant that when Jesuits are presented with two or more good options that they can be doing for God, they should try to discern which option will attract the greater number of people to him. Ignatius also called this *the more universal good* (see *SpirEx.* §23, *Cons.* §618–32).

In the *Testament*, Ignatius does not explicitly affirm that *the greater glory of God* was his core principle, but he frequently refers to God's greater glory and makes his decisions based on it (e.g., §14, 36, 57, 85). Careful readers will notice that, even when Ignatius does not refer explicitly to God's greater glory, or even when he does not refer explicitly to certain decisions that he made, nevertheless his commitment to the greater glory of God is still operative. For example, he dropped his original idea of working by himself when he realized that recruiting companions would help him make a bigger impact.

3. Discernment

Ignatius is famous for emphasizing the importance of discernment in one's relationship with God. In the *Testament*, he shares stories in which he practices two different kinds: the *discernment of spirits* and the *discernment of God's will.* Unfortunately, many who write about Ignatian discernment today fail to keep this distinction, which causes confusion. Ignatius treated them in two different sections of the *Spiritual Exercises*: §313–70 and §169–89, respectively.

Discernment of Spirits

Christians believe that God speaks to people through their thoughts, emotions, and desires. But not every thought, emotion, and desire is from God. For example, if a man shows his friends a video of a laughing baby, he can be rather sure that they will smile and get a warm feeling. But probably no one will say that the warm feeling is a message from God. It is an ordinary reaction that one can predict. But if a woman is walking down the street when she is suddenly filled with an overwhelming sense of God's love, or if she gets a recurring thought that she should be a nun, even when she tries hard not to think about it, then there is reason to believe that God is trying to tell her something.

There is a third possibility. Christians traditionally believe that the devil and other evil spirits are capable of influencing people's thoughts, emotions, and desires, for the purpose of trying to confuse them, frighten them, or otherwise lead them away from God. In the *Testament* and *Spiritual Exercises*, Ignatius calls the devil *the enemy of human nature*, or simply *the enemy.* These were old names that went back to the ancient church.

The discernment of spirits, therefore, is the process in which people analyze their own thoughts, emotions, and desires—or they analyze someone else's—in order to determine their quality and origin. Which ones come from God, which come from the enemy, and which from a human source?

Discernment of God's Will

Discerning God's will is about making choices to act. That is, when Christians have two or more good options that they can do in the service of God, which does God invite them to desire and choose? For example, the eleven apostles had to choose between two holy men, Justus and Matthias, to replace Judas (Acts of the Apostles 1:15–26). To determine what God wanted, they simply threw dice, while trusting that God would guide the outcome. Or again, St. Paul had to make a hard choice between two good options: keeping silent about his mystical experiences in order to avoid the appearance of vanity, or telling others about them in order to establish his credibility (2 Cor. 12:1–5).

Today, whenever Christians make decisions, both big and small, with an eye toward what will serve God better—*what is my vocation in the Church? What major should I choose in college? Should I gently challenge these people about their beliefs, or simply listen respectfully?*—they are trying to discern God's will.

In *A Pilgrim's Testament*, readers will find many examples of both kinds of discernment. To name just a few, Ignatius discerns the spirits when he tries to identify the source of his consolations and desolations (§8), or the true source of his seemingly good idea to make a "perfect" confession to a priest (§25), or the true origin of his vision of the serpent with many eyes (§31). Ignatius discerns God's will when he ponders whether to return to his old life or to follow Christ in a more radical way (§7), whether to join a monastery or to become a hermit (§12), and whether to cross the Mediterranean with money in his pocket or go with empty pockets in order to experience deeper trust in God (§36).

4. Mysticism

In the traditional sense of the term, a *mystic* is a person to whom God speaks in an unusually intense way. This includes dramatic experiences like visions, locutions (hearing voices), ecstasies, trances, and intellectual illuminations. When Ignatius was alive, many spiritual writers taught that the highest form of mysticism was *mystical union*. This meant that a person saw God "directly" or "face to face," so to speak, so that the person experiences a little bit of heaven while still on earth. Because mystical union is a gift from God, a Christian cannot acquire it through effort. A holy person might never experience it, whereas God might give it unexpectedly to a beginner in prayer, or even to a great sinner.

On the other hand, many writers thought it was possible for Christians to approximate, however faintly, an experience of mystical union in prayer, if they practiced their powers of concentration long enough. Imagine parents who gaze at the fingers and toes of their baby for hours and hours, without speaking and without thinking anything consciously, but still absorbed in a sense of wonder and awe. In a similar way, Christians can practice gazing upon the face of Jesus, or practice being mindful of the presence of God, without using any words or conscious thoughts, and while trying to ignore all distractions. When Ignatius was alive, writers used different terms to describe this approach to prayer. Today it is often called *acquired contemplation*, meaning that one *acquires* this contemplation through practice.

In *A Pilgrim's Testament*, Gonçalves takes pains to clarify that Ignatius was a mystic in the first sense, that is, his experiences of God went beyond anything that he could have produced as the result of his own efforts. In *Test.* §21, for example, when a holy woman says to Ignatius, "May my Lord Jesus Christ deign to appear to you someday," she perhaps meant it figuratively, but Ignatius interpreted it "quite literally." And in fact, Jesus did appear to Ignatius later in the story. Or in *Test.* §95, Gonçalves noted that Ignatius's "great supernatural visitations" (*grandi visitationi sopranaturali*) in Vicenza were the same kind that he had experienced at Manresa. In those days, *supernatural* was a semi-technical term that meant infused mystical experiences (see Ch. 10, no. 6).

Why is this distinction between *mystical union* and *acquired contemplation* important? Like countless saints before him, starting with St. Paul (2 Cor. 12:1–5), Ignatius struggled with whether to tell people about the mystical experiences he was having. But the difficulty of his struggle only makes sense if the things he wanted to share were truly extraordinary. On the one hand, he believed that telling people would strengthen their faith, and give them reason to trust him when he spoke to them about God. On the other hand, he questioned his own motives. Perhaps it was really vanity that made him want to say something. Perhaps he wanted everyone to think he was a great saint.

Once again, Ignatius stuck to his core principle: in a discernment of God's will, the deciding factor should always be the greater service of others. If he could be reasonably sure that telling others would do more good than harm, then he should tell them, even if his own motives were indeed a little mixed, and even if some people started to call him a great saint. Ignatius wrote about this in *SpirEx.* §351.

5. Pilgrimages

In the Middle Ages, Catholic Christians loved to make pilgrimages. Hundreds of sites served this purpose, but in the centuries before Ignatius, the favorite destinations were Jerusalem, Rome, the tomb of St. James the Apostle in Spain, and the tomb of St. Thomas Becket in England. Pilgrims typically wanted to win merits and indulgences, or to be cured in the waters of a holy well, or to fulfill a vow, or to find redemption or enlightenment of some kind. And because it was a time in history when the great majority of Europeans lived and died within twenty miles of where they were born, many pilgrims also wanted the adventure of a long journey from home.

For pilgrims, the benefits of the journey itself were just as important as the blessings that they hoped to obtain at the final destinations. They met others on the road who became their traveling companions, and with whom they could speak intimately about matters of faith. Pilgrims relied on the kindness of strangers for food and lodging. They also faced constant danger from hunger, thirst, injuries, infections, exhaustion, roadside bandits, pirates, sinking ships, and walking through the middle of military conflicts. As a result, pilgrims learned to put trust in God that he would take care of them, and that he truly would walk with them along the way.

Pilgrimages were also a powerful means to increase a Christian's *devotion*. This was a word that Ignatius used many times to mean a heartfelt, affective love for God and for his church. Ignatius's own devotion increased tremendously as a result of seeing all the beautiful shrines, churches, and tombs of saints on his way to Jerusalem and back. He also witnessed the reverence and piety of so many of his fellow Christians, which no doubt impressed upon him just how universal the church really is. For these reasons, Ignatius refers to pilgrimages as a means to increase devotion in *SpirEx*. §358.

Ignatius probably had not been very educated in his Catholic faith when he had his conversion experience at Castle Loyola, and he probably knew relatively little about the spiritual wisdom of the church that had been handed down for 1,500 years before him. But during the next twenty years—as he traveled from Spain to Italy to Jerusalem, and then back to Spain, France, England, and Italy—he learned much from the books that he read, the people whom he met along the way, and his personal experiences of God. And his devotion grew. Here in his *Testament*, he wants readers to see that God walks with them too, as they make their own pilgrimages.

Foreword of Fr. Jerónimo Nadal

St. Ignatius entrusted Jerónimo Nadal with visiting new Jesuit communities throughout Europe, in order to teach priests, scholastics (seminarians), and brothers about Ignatius's values and the distinctiveness of the Jesuit vocation. Nadal's lecture notes, and his commentaries on the Jesuit Constitutions, *are critical sources for understanding early Jesuit spirituality.*

Apparently, Nadal did not know that Gonçalves had already written a foreword to Ignatius's Testament, *and so he composed this one, probably sometime between 1561 and 1567 (see* FontNarr. *1:344–46). The Latin original of his foreword is in* FontNarr. *1:354–63.*

I myself and other fathers had heard from our Father Ignatius that he had asked God to grant him three blessings before he departed from this life. First, the confirmation of the Institute of the Society by the Apostolic See. Second, the confirmation of the *Spiritual Exercises*. Third, to write the *Constitutions*.

As I was mindful of this, and saw that he had obtained them all, I was afraid, lest he be called away from us to a better life. Since I knew also that the holy fathers, founders of monastic institutes,[1] had a custom of leaving to their sons, by way of a testament,[2] those counsels that they believed would help toward their perfection in virtue, I awaited the opportune moment to request the same of Father Ignatius. In 1551, it happened that we were together, and Father Ignatius said: "Just now I was higher than heaven."[3] I gathered that he had had some kind of ecstasy or rapture, as he was frequently wont. With the greatest respect, I asked: "What was it, father?" But he changed the subject.

Judging this to be an opportune moment, I requested and begged the father to explain to us how God had guided him from the beginning of his conversion, in such a way that this explanation could serve us as a sort of testament and paternal instruction. "Because," I said to him, "now that you have obtained those three things, father, that you had desired to see before death, we are afraid that you will be taken up into heaven."

The father cited his responsibilities as an excuse, saying that these did not permit him to give time or attention to it. However, he said, "Celebrate three Masses about this matter—Polanco, Ponce, and yourself—and tell me what you think after prayer."[4] I said to him: "Father, we shall think exactly what we think now." He added very gently, "Do as I say." We celebrated the Masses, and gave him the same opinion. He promised to do what we asked. The following year, upon returning from Sicily once again to be sent to Spain, I asked the father if he had done anything. "Nothing," he said. I again asked on returning from Spain in 1554. He had not started.

Then, moved by I know not what spirit, I said with firmness to the father,

> It has been four years since I asked you, not in my name only, but in that of the other fathers, to explain to us how the Lord formed you since the beginning of your conversion. We are convinced that this will be useful, principally for us and for the Society. But as I see that you are not doing it, I dare to assure you this: if you do what we so much desire, we shall use such a blessing most diligently; but if you do not, we shall not be disheartened, but we will be as confident in the Lord as if you had written everything.

The father made no reply, but called Father Luís Gonçalves— that same day, I think—and began to relate to him the things that Fr. Luís with his excellent memory later wrote down.[5] These are the *Acta Patris Ignatii* that are in circulation.[6] Father Luís was an elector in the First General Congregation, and there he was elected assistant to Superior General Father Laínez. A father outstanding in religious spirit and virtue, he later educated Sebastian, the king of Portugal, in letters and Christian virtues.[7]

Father Gonçalves wrote partly in Spanish, partly in Italian, as scribes were available. Father Hannibal du Coudret, a learned and devout father, made a Latin translation. Both author and translator are still alive.[8]

Foreword of Fr. Luís Gonçalves da Câmara

Luís Gonçalves da Câmara was a Portuguese Jesuit from an aristocratic family. After caring for slaves in Portugal and North Africa, he was sent to Rome, where he met his hero Ignatius at the Society's headquarters. He wrote an account of Ignatius's daily activities from January 26 to October 18, 1555. This Memoriale, *as it is known today, provides an invaluable window into the saint's personality, and how he applied his spiritual principles in concrete situations.*

Gonçalves wrote his foreword in Rome (Eaglestone §110). That he does not mention Ignatius's death suggests he was still alive; this would place the probable date of composition in the last weeks before Gonçalves left for Portugal on October 23, 1555. The Spanish original and Latin translation are found in FontNarr. *1:354–63.*

One Friday morning in the year 1553, the fourth of August, on the eve of Our Lady of Snows, while the father was in the garden by the house or apartment known as the duke's, I began to give him an account of some particulars concerning my soul. Among other things, I spoke to him of vainglory. As a remedy, the father told me to refer everything of mine frequently to God, striving to offer him all the good I found in myself, acknowledging it as his and giving him thanks for it. He spoke to me about this in a manner that greatly consoled me, so that I could not restrain my tears.[2] Thus the father told me how much he had been bothered by this vice for two years, so much so, that when he embarked from Barcelona for Jerusalem, he did not dare to tell anyone that he was going to Jerusalem; and so in other similar instances. And he went on to say how much peace of soul he then felt in this regard.

An hour or two after this, we went inside for supper. While Master Polanco and I were eating with him, the father said that Master Nadal and others of the Society had often asked something of him, and he had never made up his mind about it. But, after having spoken with me, when he had retired to his room, he had such a devout inclination to do it, and—he was speaking in a manner that showed that God had greatly enlightened him as to his duty to do so[3]—that he was fully decided on this, that he would narrate all that occurred in his soul until now. He had also decided that I should be the one to whom he would reveal these things.

The father was very ill at that time, and he never would promise himself a single day of life. Rather, if someone says, "I will do this fifteen days from now," or "eight days from now," the father always says as if he were surprised, "What, do you think that you will live that long?"[4] Nevertheless, this time, he said that he expected to live three or four months in order to finish this business. The next day, I spoke to him, asking when he wished us to begin. He replied that I should remind him of it each day—I do not remember how many days—until he was in a position to do it. But putting it off because of business, he later arranged that I remind him each Sunday. So in September—I do not remember how many days had passed— the father called me and began to tell me about his whole life, and his youthful transgressions, clearly and distinctly, and with all the details.[5] Later that same month, he called me three or four times—as can be seen by the difference in handwriting[6]—and he continued his story down to his early days.

The father's narrative style is the same that he uses in everything.[7] He speaks with such clarity that he makes all that has passed seem as if it is happening right now. Therefore, it was not necessary to ask him anything more, because the father remembered to say everything that would help one to understand. Then, without saying anything to the father, I went immediately to write it down, first in notes by my own hand, and later at greater length, as it is written here. I have endeavored not to put down any words except those I heard from the father. And regarding those places where I fear that I have failed, it is that, in order not to depart from the father's words, I have not been able to explain clearly the force of some of them.

Thus I was writing this, as indicated above, until September 1553. But from then until Father Nadal came on October 8, 1554, the father was always excusing himself because of some illness, or various affairs on hand, saying to me, "When that affair is over, remind me of it." And when it was over, and I reminded him of it, he would say, "We are now engaged in this other matter. When it is over, remind me of it."

When Father Nadal came, he was very pleased that it was begun. But he asked me to urge the father, telling me many times that the father could do nothing of greater benefit for the Society than this, and that this was truly to found the Society. He himself spoke to me to remind him of it, when the business of endowing the Roman College was finished. But after it was done, [he asked to delay again], until the affair of Prester John was finished and the mail had gone.[8]

We got going with the story on the ninth of March, but Pope Julius III began to be in a serious condition at that time, and died on the twenty-third. So the father postponed the matter until there was a pope. But then, this pope also fell ill and died (that was Marcellus).[9] The father delayed until the election of Pope Paul IV.[10] And then, because of the great heat and his many engagements, he postponed it repeatedly until the twenty-first of September, when my being sent to Spain began to be discussed. For this reason, I strongly pressed the father to fulfill his promise to me. So now, he arranged to do it on the morning of the twenty-second, in the Red Tower.[11] Accordingly, when I had finished saying Mass, I presented myself to him to ask if it was time.

He replied that I should wait for him in the Red Tower, so that when he arrived, I would be there. I took it to mean that I would have to wait for him a long time in that place. As I waited on a porch, speaking with a brother who had asked me something, the father came along and chastised me because, failing in obedience, I had not waited for him in the Red Tower. So he did not want to do anything that day.

Later we were again very insistent with him. So he returned to the Red Tower, and dictated while pacing about, as he had always done before. In order to observe his face, I kept moving a little closer to him, but the father said to me, "Keep the rule."[12] When, forgetting his remark, I drew closer to him—I made that mistake two or three times—the father called it to my attention, and walked off. Finally, he returned to the same tower and finished dictating to me what is written down here. But as I was for some time already on the point of undertaking my journey—for the eve of my departure was the last day on which the father spoke to me about this matter—I was unable to write out everything in Rome. And not having a Spanish scribe in Genoa, I dictated in Italian whatever I had brought in summary from Rome. I finished the writing in Genoa in December 1555.

A Pilgrim's Testament

Iñigo López de Loyola was born in Loyola Castle on the outskirts of the village of Azpeitia, in the Basque province of Guipúzcoa in northeastern Spain. As the youngest of thirteen children, he did not stand to inherit anything of the family estate, but he was still a hidalgo (nobleman), meaning that political connections remained important. At sixteen, his family sent him to Arévalo to work as a page in the service of Juan Velásquez de Cuellar, the royal treasurer. Iñigo lived with Velásquez's twelve children for ten years, learning horseback riding, sword fighting, and courtly etiquette.

Velásquez died in 1517. His widow sent Iñigo to the duke of Nájera, Don Antonio Manrique de Lara, viceroy of Navarre. There he worked three years as a successful gentleman-diplomat. He also frittered his time in duels, tournaments, gambling, and philandering. He was not a soldier properly so-called, but the duke could call upon him to fight. In 1521, a French army of twelve thousand infantry, eight hundred lancers, and twenty-nine pieces of artillery advanced on the fortress at Pamplona near the French–Spanish border, with the intention of penetrating into the heart of Spain. To defend the fortress, the duke could summon only three thousand infantry and seven hundred horses. On May 17, Iñigo hastened to Pamplona to help defend it.

1. Pamplona and Loyola (May 1521 to Late February 1522)

[1] Until the age of twenty-six, he was a man given to the vanities of the world.[1] What he enjoyed most was the exercise of arms, having a great and foolish desire to win fame.

And when he was in a fortress that the French were attacking,[2] all were of the view that they should surrender in order to save their lives, for they saw clearly that they could not offer resistance. But he gave so many reasons to the commander, that he actually persuaded him to resist, even though it was contrary to the opinion of all the officers, who nevertheless drew courage from his spirit and determination.

When the day came on which they expected the bombardment, he confessed to one of those companions in arms.[3] After the bombardment had lasted a good while, a shot struck him on one leg, shattering it completely. And because the cannon ball passed between both legs, the other one was badly injured.[4]

[2] Shortly after his fall, those in the fortress surrendered to the French, who, upon taking possession of it, treated the wounded man very well, with courtesy and kindness. After he had been in Pamplona for twelve or fifteen days, they carried him home to his native land in a litter.[5]

At home, he was in a bad way. Summoning doctors and surgeons from all over the area, they judged that the leg should be broken again, and the bones reset. They said that the bones were set badly the first time, or perhaps they had been jostled apart again on the road. Since they were out of place, he could not mend properly. So he submitted to this butchery once again. Meanwhile, he never said a word, nor showed any sign of pain, other than to clench his fists tightly. He did likewise in all the other butcheries before or after that he underwent.[6]

[3] Yet he kept getting worse, not being able to eat, and he showed the other symptoms that usually point to death. When the feast day of St.

John came, he was advised to make a confession, because the doctors were far from confident about his health. He received the sacraments on the eve of the feast day of Saints Peter and Paul.[7] The doctors said that if he did not feel better by midnight, he could be taken for dead. But it happened that this sick man was devoted to St. Peter, so Our Lord deigned that he should begin to get better that very midnight. His improvement was so rapid, that some days later they judged him to be out of danger of death.

[4] But when his bones knit together, one bone below the knee was sitting on top of the other, which made the leg shorter. The bone protruded so much that it was ugly. He could not bear such a thing, because he had his heart set on a worldly career, and he thought that this would deform him. He asked the surgeons if they could cut it off. They said that they could, but the pain would be greater than everything that he had suffered previously, because the bone was already healed, and it would take a while to cut it. And yet he freely chose on his own to be martyred, even though his elder brother was shocked, and said that he himself would not dare to suffer such pain. But the wounded man endured it with his normal patience.[8]

[5] After they cut away the flesh and excess bone, corrective measures were taken that the leg might not be short. Ointment was often applied, and it was stretched continually with instruments that tortured him for many days. But Our Lord continued to sustain his health, so that he found himself fit in all other respects, except that he could not stand easily on the leg, so that he was obliged to stay in bed.

And as he was much given to reading worldly books of fiction, commonly labeled chivalry, on feeling well, he asked to be given some of them to pass the time. But in that house none of those that he usually read could be found, so they gave him a Life of Christ and a book of the lives of the saints in Castilian.[9]

[6] As he read them many times, he became rather fond of what he found written there. But interrupting his reading, he sometimes stopped to think about the things that he had read. At other times, he thought about the things of the world, about which he had been in the habit of musing earlier. Of the many foolish ideas that occurred to him, one took such a hold on his heart, that without realizing it, he was absorbed in thinking about it for two, three, or four hours. He imagined what he would do in the service of a certain lady: the means that he would take to reach the land where she lived, the witty things he would say, the words he would use when speaking to her, the feats of arms that he would perform in her service. He became so infatuated with all this that he did not stop to think how impossible it was to do it, because the lady was not of the ordinary nobility. She was neither a countess nor a duchess, but her position was higher than any of these.[10]

[7] Nevertheless, Our Lord assisted him, causing other thoughts to follow these, thoughts that arose from the things he read.[11] For in reading the life of Our Lord, and of the saints, he stopped to think, reasoning within himself: "What if I should do this which St. Francis did? And this which St. Dominic did?"[12] Thus he pondered over many things that he found good, always proposing to himself what was difficult and burdensome. But to him, it seemed easy for him to accomplish it. But he did not do anything more than have a conversation within himself, saying, "St. Dominic did this, so I have to do it. St. Francis did this, so I have to do it."[13]

These thoughts also lasted a long time. Then, the worldly ones mentioned above returned, interspersing themselves with the good thoughts. He stayed long with them, also. This succession of diverse thoughts lasted for quite some time. He always dwelled at length upon whatever thought came to him, either regarding the worldly feats that he wished to perform, or the others for God that came to his imagination, until he would tire of it all, and put it aside, and turn to other matters.

[8] Yet there was this difference. When he was thinking of those things of the world, he took much delight in them. But afterward, when he was tired and put them aside, he found himself dry and dissatisfied. Yet when he thought about going to Jerusalem barefoot, and about eating nothing but plain vegetables, and about practicing all the other rigors that he saw the saints had done,[14] not only was he consoled when he had these thoughts, but even after putting them aside he remained satisfied and joyful.[15]

He did not notice it at first, nor did he stop to ponder the distinction. But then, his eyes were opened a little, and he began to wonder at the difference, and to reflect upon it, realizing from experience that some thoughts left him sad, and others joyful. Little by little, he came to recognize the difference between the spirits that were stirring: one from the devil, the other from God.[16]

[9] From this lesson, he derived not a little light. He began to think more earnestly about his past life and about the great need he had to do penance for it. At this point, the desire to imitate the saints came to him, although he gave no thought to the details. He only promised that, with God's grace, he would do as they had done. But the one thing he did want, as he mentioned above, was to go to Jerusalem as soon as he recovered, and to do it with as many disciplines and fasts as a generous spirit, on fire with God, would want to perform.

[10] And so he began to forget the previous thoughts, with these holy desires he had. They were confirmed by a visitation, in this manner. One night while he was awake, he saw clearly an image of Our Lady with the holy Child Jesus. From this sight, he received for a considerable time an over-abundance of consolation,[17] and he was left with such loathing for his whole past life, and especially for the things of the flesh, that it seemed to him that his soul was rid of all the species that had been painted on it.[18] Thus, from that hour until August 1553, when this was written, he never gave the slightest consent to the things of the flesh.[19] For this reason, it may be considered the

work of God,[20] although he did not dare to claim it, nor said more than to affirm the above. But his brother as well as all the rest of the household came to know from his exterior the change that had taken place in his soul.

[11] With no worry at all, he persevered in his reading and his good resolutions.[21] In all his conversations with members of the household, he spoke on the things of God. Thus he benefited their souls. As he very much liked those books, the idea came to him to note down briefly some of the more essential things from the life of Christ and the saints.[22] So he set himself very diligently to write a book—because he was now beginning to be up and about the house a bit—with red ink for the words of Christ, and blue ink for those of Our Lady. He did it on polished and lined paper, and with good handwriting, because he was a very fine penman.[23]

He spent part of his time in writing, and part in prayer. The greatest consolation he experienced was gazing at the sky and the stars, which he often did, and for a long time. By doing so, he felt within himself a very great impulse to serve Our Lord. He often thought about his resolution, and he wished that he were now completely well, so he could get on his way.[24]

[12] After taking stock of what he might do after he returned from Jerusalem, so he could always live as a penitent, he thought he might enter the Carthusian house in Seville,[25] without saying who he was, so that they would make little of him.[26] There, he would never eat anything except plain vegetables. But when he thought again of the penances he wished to do as he went about the world, the desire to enter the Carthusians cooled. He feared that he would not be able to give vent to the hatred that he had conceived against himself. Nevertheless, he instructed one of the household servants who was going to Burgos to get information about the rule of the Carthusians. The information that he obtained about it seemed good.

But for the reason mentioned above, and because he was wholly preoccupied with the journey that he was planning to make soon, and also because the matter did not have to be decided until his return, he did not much look into it. Rather, finding now that he had some strength, he thought the time to depart had come. He said to his brother, "Sir, the duke of Nájera, as you know, is aware that I am now well. It will be good that I go to Navarrete." (The duke was there at that time.)[27]

His brother took him from one room to another, and with much feeling, begged him not to throw himself away, and to consider the hopes that people had placed in him, and how much he could achieve. He said many such things, all for the purpose of dissuading him from his good desire.[28] But he answered in such a way that, without departing from the truth—for he was now very scrupulous about that—he slipped away from his brother.[29]

2. Road to Montserrat (February to March 1522)

[13] And so, as he mounted a mule, another brother wished to go with him as far as Oñate.[1] On the road, he persuaded him to join him in a vigil at Our Lady of Aránzazu. That night, he prayed there that he might gain fresh strength for his journey.[2] He left his brother in Oñate, at the house of a sister he was going to visit. Then he continued to Navarrete.[3]

Remembering that a few ducats were owed him at the duke's household, he thought it would be a good idea to collect them. So he wrote out a bill for the treasurer. The treasurer said that he had no money. The duke, upon hearing this, said that even if he had nothing, he would not fail to give something to Loyola. He wanted to give him a good position, if he would accept it, because of the reputation that he had earned in the past.

He collected the money, and arranged that it be distributed among certain persons to whom he felt indebted, with a portion going to a statue of Our Lady that was deteriorated, so that it could be repaired and handsomely adorned. Then, dismissing the two servants who had come with him, he set out alone on his mule from Navarrete to Montserrat.

[14] On the way, something happened to him that would be good to record,[4] so one may understand how Our Lord dealt with this soul, which was still blind, though greatly desirous of serving him as far as his knowledge went.[5] Thus, he decided to do great penances, no longer with an eye to satisfying for his sins, so much as to please and gratify God. So when it occurred to him to do some penance that the saints practiced, he determined to do the same, and even more.[6]

From these thoughts, he derived all his consolation, not looking to any interior thing, nor knowing what was humility or charity or patience, or the discernment that regulates and measures these virtues.[7] His whole intention was to do such great external works because the saints had done so for the glory of God, without looking to any more particular consideration.[8]

[15] Well, as he was going on his way, a Moor riding on a mule caught up with him.[9] They went along conversing together, and got to talking about Our Lady. The Moor said it seemed to him that the Virgin had indeed conceived without a man, but he could not believe that she gave birth while remaining a virgin.[10] In support of this, he cited the natural arguments that suggested themselves to him.[11] The pilgrim, despite the many reasons that he gave him, could not change his opinion. The Moor then went ahead so quickly that he lost sight of him, and he was left pondering over what had transpired with the Moor.

At this, various emotions came over him, and caused discontent in his soul, as it seemed that he had not done his duty. They also aroused his indignation against the Moor, for it seemed that he had done wrong in allowing the Moor to say such things about Our Lady, and that he ought to charge forward in defense of her honor. He felt inclined to search for the Moor and stab him for what he had said. Persevering a long time in the conflict caused by those desires, he remained unsure at the end, not knowing what he ought to do. The Moor, who had moved ahead, had told him that he was going to a place a little farther on the same road, very near the highway, though the highway did not pass through the place.

[16] So, being tired of examining what would be best to do, and not arriving at a definite conclusion, he decided as follows: to let the mule go with reins slack as far as the place where the roads parted. And if the mule took the village road, he would find the Moor and stab him. If the mule did not go toward the village, but took the highway, then he would let him be.[12] He acted upon that thought. Our Lord deigned that although the village was a little more than thirty or forty paces away, and the road to it was very broad and maintained, the mule took the highway instead, and left the village road.

Coming to a large town before Montserrat, he decided to buy there the attire that he had resolved to wear when going to Jerusalem. He bought cloth from which sacks are usually made, loosely woven and very prickly. Then he ordered a long garment to be made from it that extended to his feet. He bought a pilgrim's staff and a small gourd, and put everything in front, by the mule's saddle.[13]

[17] He went on his way to Montserrat, thinking as he always did of the exploits he would perform for the love of God. And as his mind was all full of tales like *Amadís de Gaula* and such books, the ideas that came to him were along those lines.[14] Thus he decided to keep a vigil of arms one whole night, without sitting or lying down.[15] He alternated between standing and kneeling before the altar of Our Lady of Montserrat. There, he resolved to lay aside his [noble] garments, and to put on the armor of Christ. So leaving this place, he set off, thinking as usual of his resolutions.

Upon his arrival in Montserrat, he prayed and made an appointment with the confessor, to whom he made a general confession in writing.[16] It lasted three days. He made arrangements with the confessor to have someone take his mule, and to have his sword and dagger placed in the church, at the altar of Our Lady.[17] This was the first man to whom he revealed his purpose, because until then, he had not revealed it to any confessor.[18]

[18] In March 1522, on the eve of Our Lady, at night, he went as secretly as he could to a beggar, and stripping off all his garments, he gave them to him. He dressed himself in his chosen attire and went to kneel before the altar of Our Lady. At times in this way, at other times standing, with his pilgrim's staff in his hand, he spent the whole night.

He left at daybreak so as not to be recognized. He did not take the road that led straight to Barcelona, where he would come across many who would recognize and honor him,[19] but instead turned toward a town called Manresa. Here he planned to stay in a hospice a few days,[20] as well as to note some things in his book. This he carried around very carefully, and it consoled him greatly.

After he had gone a few miles from Montserrat, a man who had been chasing after him finally caught up. He asked the pilgrim if he had given some clothes to a beggar, as the beggar had claimed. Answering that he had, tears flowed from the pilgrim's eyes in compassion for the beggar to whom he had given the clothing. He realized that they were harassing him, thinking that he had stolen them.

Yet as much as he avoided favorable notice, he could not remain long in Manresa before people had a big story to tell—their ideas coming from what happened at Montserrat. Soon, the tale grew into saying more than the truth: that he had given up a large income, etc.[21]

3. Sojourn at Manresa (March 1522 to February 1523)

[19] He begged alms in Manresa every day. He neither ate meat nor drank wine, even though they were offered to him. He did not fast on Sundays, and if they gave him a little wine, he drank it. Because he had been very fastidious about taking care of his hair, as was the fashion at that time—and his was handsome—he decided to let it grow wild, without combing it, or cutting it, or covering it with anything at night or day. For the same reason, he let the nails grow on his toes and fingers, because he had been fastidious about this too.[1]

While in this hospice, it often happened that in broad daylight he saw something in the air near him. It gave him great consolation because it was very beautiful, remarkably so. He could not discern very well the kind of thing it was, but in a way, it seemed to him to have the form of a serpent with many things that shone like eyes, though they were not. He found great pleasure and consolation in seeing this thing, and the more often he saw it, the more his consolation grew. When it disappeared, he was displeased.[2]

[20] Until this time, he always persevered in nearly the same interior state of very steady joy, without having any knowledge of interior things of the spirit. In the days while that vision lasted, or somewhat before it began—for it lasted many days—there came a forceful thought that troubled him, pointing out the hardships of his life, as if they were saying within his soul,[3] "How will you be able to endure this life for the seventy years you have to live?"[4] Sensing that it was from the enemy, he answered interiorly with great vehemence, "Wretch! Can you promise me an hour of life?"[5] So he overcame the temptation and remained at peace. This was the first temptation that came to him after what is mentioned above.[6] It happened when he was entering a church where he heard High Mass each day, and Vespers, and Compline. All these were sung, which comforted him greatly. At Mass, he usually read the Passion, always retaining his serenity.

[21] But soon after the temptation noted above, he began to feel great changes in his soul. Sometimes he felt so out of sorts that he found no relish in saying prayers, nor in hearing Mass, nor in any other devotion that he might practice. At other times, quite the opposite came over him, and so suddenly that he seemed to have thrown off sadness and desolation, just as one snatches a cape from another's shoulders.[7] Now he started getting perturbed by the changes that he had never experienced before, and he said to himself, "What new life is this, that we are now beginning?"

At this time, he still conversed occasionally with spiritual persons who had regard for him, and who wanted to talk to him. This was because in his speech he revealed great fervor and eagerness to advance in God's service, even though he did not yet have any knowledge of spiritual matters. At that time, there was at Manresa a woman of great age, with a long record also as a servant of God, and known as such in many parts of Spain.[8] So much so, that the Catholic king once summoned her to communicate something. One day this woman, speaking to the new soldier of Christ,[9] said to him, "Oh! May my Lord Jesus Christ deign to appear to you some day." But he was startled at this, taking the matter quite literally, "How would Jesus Christ appear to me?" He persevered steadily in his usual confession and Communion each Sunday.

[22] But here he began to have much trouble from scruples.[10] Even though the general confession he made at Montserrat had been done quite carefully—and all in writing, as he said earlier—still at times it seemed to him that he had failed to confess certain things. This caused him much distress, because although he confessed that too, he was not satisfied.[11] Thus, he began to look for some spiritual men who could cure him of these scruples, but nothing helped.[12] Finally, a doctor of the cathedral, a very spiritual man who preached there, told him one day in confession to write down everything he could remember. He did so, but after confession, the scruples returned, and became increasingly nit-picky, so that he was in great distress.

Although he was practically convinced that those scruples did him much harm, and that it would be good to get rid of them, he could not free himself from them. Sometimes he thought it would cure him if his confessor ordered him in the name of Jesus Christ not to confess anything of the past. He wanted his confessor to order him in this way, but he did not dare say it to his confessor.

[23] But without his saying so, his confessor ordered him not to confess anything of the past, unless it was something quite clear. But since he found all those things to be very clear, this order was of no use to him. And so he continued with the difficulty. At this time, he was staying in a small room that the Dominicans had given him in their monastery. He persevered in his seven hours of prayer on his knees, getting up regularly at midnight, and in all the other exercises mentioned earlier. But in none of them did he find any cure for his scruples. They were tormenting him for many months.

Once, when he was very distressed by them, he began to pray. Roused to fervor, he shouted aloud to God, saying,

Help me, Lord, for I find no remedy in people, nor in any creature. Yet, if I thought I could find it, no labor would be too hard for me. Yourself, Lord, show me where I may find it. Even if I have to chase after a puppy that it may give me the remedy, I will do it.

[24] While he had these thoughts, the temptation often came over him with great force to throw himself from a large balcony in his room,[13] next to the place where he was praying. But realizing that it was a sin to kill oneself, he shouted again, "Lord, I will do nothing that offends you," repeating these words many times, as well as the previous ones. Then there came to his mind the story of a saint who, in order to obtain from God something that he wanted very much, refused to eat for many days, until he got it.[14] Thinking about this for a good while, he at last decided to do it, telling himself that he would not eat nor drink until God came to his aid, or unless he saw that his

death was quite close. For if it happened that he found himself at the extreme limit, so that he would soon die if he did not eat, then he would ask for bread, and to eat—provided that he would even be able to ask, or to eat, at that extreme limit.

[25] This happened one Sunday after he had received Communion. He persevered the whole week without putting anything into his mouth. He did not cease his usual exercises, even going to divine office and saying his prayers on his knees, even at midnight, etc. But when the next Sunday came, and he had to go to confession, since he used to tell his confessor in great detail what he had done, he also told him how he had eaten nothing during that week. His confessor ordered him to break that fast. Even though he still felt strong, he nevertheless obeyed his confessor. That day and the next, he felt free from scruples. But on the third day, which was Tuesday, while at prayer, he began to remember his sins again. And since one thing leads to another, he went on thinking of sin after sin from his past, so that he felt like he was obliged to confess them again.

But after these thoughts, disgust for the life he led came over him, with impulses to give it up.[15] In this way, the Lord deigned that he awake as if from sleep.[16] As he now had some experience of the diversity of spirits from the lessons God had given him, he began to examine the means by which that spirit had come.[17] He thus decided with great lucidity not to confess anything from the past any more. From that day forward, he remained free of those scruples, and he held it for certain that Our Lord had mercifully deigned to deliver him.

[26] Besides his seven hours of prayer,[18] he busied himself helping certain souls who came there looking for him, with regard to spiritual matters. All the rest of the day, he spent thinking about the things of God that he had meditated upon or read that day. But when he went to bed, great enlightenment and spiritual consolations often came to him, so that they made him lose much of the time he had

allotted to sleep, which was not much. Examining this several times, he thought to himself that he had already dedicated ample time to conversing with God, and all the rest of the day as well. He began to doubt, therefore, that the enlightenment came from a good spirit.[19] He concluded that it would be better to ignore it, and to sleep for the allotted time. And so he did.

[27] He persevered in his abstention from meat. He was so determined about it that he would not think of changing it for any reason. But one day, when he got up in the morning, edible meat appeared before him, as if he saw it with his ordinary eyes, although no desire for it had preceded this. At the same time, he also had a strong inclination of his will to eat it from then on. Although he remembered his previous resolution, he nevertheless had no doubt about this, but rather a conviction that he should eat meat. Later, on reporting this to his confessor, the confessor told him to consider whether perhaps this was a temptation. But examining it carefully, he could never doubt it.[20]

God treated him at this time just as a schoolmaster treats a child whom he is teaching.[21] Whether this was because of his lack of education and of brains, or because he had no one to teach him, or because of the strong desire that God himself had given him to serve him, he believed without doubt, and has always believed, that God treated him in this way. Indeed, if he were to doubt this, he would think he offended his Divine Majesty. Something of this can be seen from the five following points.[22]

[28] *First*: he had great devotion to the Most Holy Trinity, and so each day he prayed to the three Persons separately. But as he also prayed to the Most Holy Trinity, the thought came to him: Why did he have to say four prayers to the Trinity? But this thought gave him little or no difficulty, being hardly important. One day, while saying the Office of Our Lady on the steps of the same monastery, his understanding began to be elevated, as though he saw the Most Holy Trinity in the form of three musical keys. This provoked so many tears and

so much sobbing that he could not control himself. That morning, while joining in a procession that set out from there, he could not hold back his tears until dinnertime. Nor, after eating, could he stop talking about the Most Holy Trinity, for which purpose he used a great variety of comparisons, and with much joy and consolation. As a result, throughout his life, a feeling of great devotion came over him whenever he prayed to the Most Holy Trinity.[23]

[29] *Second*: once, the manner in which God had created the world was presented to his understanding with great spiritual joy. He seemed to see something white, from which some rays were coming, and God made light from these. But he did not know how to explain these things, nor did he remember too well the spiritual enlightenment that God was imprinting on his soul at the time.

Third: at Manresa too, where he stayed almost a year, after he began to be consoled by God, and saw the fruit that he bore in dealing with souls, he gave up those extremes he had formerly practiced. Now, he cut his nails and his hair. One day in this town, while he was hearing Mass in the church of the monastery mentioned above, at the elevation of the Body of the Lord, he saw with interior eyes something like white rays coming from above. Although he cannot explain this very well after so long a time, nevertheless, what he saw clearly with his understanding was how Jesus Christ Our Lord was there in that Most Holy Sacrament.

Fourth: often and for a long time, while at prayer, he saw with interior eyes the humanity of Christ. The form that appeared to him was like a white body, neither very large nor very small, but he did not see any distinction of members. He saw it at Manresa many times. If he should say twenty or forty, he would not dare judge it a lie. He has seen this another time in Jerusalem and yet another while traveling near Padua. He has also seen Our Lady in a similar form, without distinguishing parts.

These things that he saw strengthened him then, and always gave him such strength in his faith. He has often thought to himself that if there were no scriptures to teach us these matters of faith, he would be resolved to die for them, solely because of what he has seen.[24]

[30] *Fifth*: once, in a spirit of devotion, he was going to a church situated a little more than a mile from Manresa. I believe it is called St. Paul's, and the road goes by the river. As he went along, occupied with his devotions, he sat down for a little while with his face toward the river, which ran down below. While he was seated there, the eyes of his understanding began to be opened. He did not see any vision, but he understood and learned many things, both spiritual matters and matters of faith and of scholarship, and this with so great an enlightenment that everything seemed new to him.[25]

The details that he understood then, though there were many, cannot be stated, except that he experienced a great clarity in his understanding. This was such that, in the whole course of his life, after completing sixty-two years, even if he gathered up all the various helps he may have had from God, and all the various things he has known, even adding them all together, he does not think he had got as much as at that one time.

[31] After this had lasted for a good while, he went to kneel before a nearby cross to give thanks to God. There, the vision that had appeared to him many times, but that he had never understood, that is, the thing mentioned above that seemed very beautiful to him, with many eyes, now appeared to him. But while before the cross, he saw clearly that the object did not have its usual beautiful color, and he knew very clearly, with a strong agreement of his will, that it was the devil. Later it would often appear to him for a long time. As a show of contempt, he dispelled it with a staff that he used to carry in his hand.

[32] Once while he was ill at Manresa, a very severe fever brought him to the point of death. He fully believed that his soul was about to leave him. At this, a thought came to him, telling him that he was

a just man, but this caused him so much trouble that he constantly rejected it, and he called his sins to mind. He had more trouble with this thought than with the fever itself. But no matter how much trouble he took to overcome the thought, he could not do so. Then, when he was somewhat relieved of the fever, and he was no longer at the point of expiring, he began to shout loudly to some ladies who had come there to visit him, that for the love of God, when they next saw him at the point of death, they should shout at him with loud voices, addressing him as a sinner. They should make him remember the offenses that he had committed against God.[26]

[33] Another time, while going by sea from Valencia to Italy in a violent storm, the rudder of the ship was broken. The situation reached such a pass that, in his judgment and that of many others who sailed on the ship, they would not be able to escape death without divine intervention. At this time, examining himself carefully and preparing to die, he could not feel afraid for his sins, or of being condemned. But he did feel embarrassment and sorrow, as he believed he had not used well the gifts and graces that God Our Lord had granted him.[27]

Another time, in the year 1550, he was in a grave state from a very severe illness. In his opinion and that of many others, it would be his last. On this occasion, thinking about death, he felt such joy and such spiritual consolation at having to die, that he dissolved entirely into tears. This became so habitual that he often stopped thinking about death, so as not to feel so much of that consolation.

[34] When winter came, he came down with a very severe illness. For treatment, the town put him in a house of the father of one Ferrera, who was later in the service of Balthasar de Faria. There he was cared for with great attention. Many prominent ladies, because of the deep regard they now had for him, came to watch over him by night. Although he recovered from this illness, he was still very weak and had frequent stomach pains.[28] For these reasons, and because the winter was very cold, they made him dress better, and wear shoes,

and cover his head. This included two brown jackets of very coarse cloth, and a cap of the same, something like a beret. At this time, there was a long period during which he was eager to converse on spiritual matters, and to find persons who could deal with them. Meantime, the time was approaching when he planned to set out for Jerusalem.

[35] At the beginning of the year 1523, he set out for Barcelona, to take a ship from there. Although there were some offers of company, he wanted to go quite alone, for his whole idea was to have God alone as refuge. One day when some were urging strongly, because he did not know either the Italian or the Latin languages, that he have a certain companion, telling him how much this would help him and praising the person highly, he said that he would not go even in the company of the son or the brother of the duke of Cardona, because he wanted to practice three virtues: charity, faith, and hope. If he took a companion, he would expect help from him when he was hungry; if he fell down, the man would help him get up; and so also he would trust him and feel attachment to him on this account. Instead, he wanted to place that trust, attachment, and expectation in God alone.

What he said in this way, he felt just so in his heart. With these thoughts, he not only had the desire to set out alone but also to go without any provisions. When he began to arrange for his passage, he prevailed upon the master of the ship to take him for free, as he had no money. But the master set a condition that he bring some biscuits for his sustenance. Otherwise, they would not take him for anything in the world.

[36] When he went to obtain the biscuits, great scruples came over him: "Is this the hope and faith you had in God who would not fail you?" etc. This was so powerful as to trouble him greatly. At last, not knowing what to do because he saw probable reasons on both sides, he decided to place himself in the hands of his confessor. So he told him how much he wanted to seek perfection, and that which would be more for the glory of God, and the reasons that caused him to doubt

whether he ought to take any provisions. The confessor decided that he should beg what was necessary and take it with him.

As he begged from a lady, she asked where he was planning to travel. He hesitated a bit whether he would tell her, but at last he ventured to say no more than that he was going to Italy and to Rome.[29] She replied, as if amazed, "You want to go to Rome? Well, I don't know how those who go there come back." (She meant to say that in Rome one profited little in spiritual things.) Now, the reason why he did not dare say that he was going to Jerusalem was fear of vainglory. This fear haunted him so much, that he never dared say to what country or to what family he belonged. At last, having the biscuit, he went on board. But at the shore he found he had five or six *blancas* left from what he was given begging from door to door (for he used to live that way). He left them on a bench that he came across there by the shore.

[37] So he embarked, having been in Barcelona a little more than twenty days. Before embarking, while he was still in Barcelona, he sought out, as was his practice, all spiritual persons, even though they lived in hermitages far from the city, to converse with them.[30] But neither in Barcelona nor in Manresa, during the whole time he was there, did he find persons who could help him as much as he wished. Only in Manresa did he find that woman whom he mentioned above, who told him that she prayed to God that Jesus Christ might appear to him. She alone seemed to him to enter more deeply into spiritual matters. Thus, after leaving Barcelona, he completely lost this eagerness to seek out spiritual persons.

4. Pilgrimage to Jerusalem (March to September 1523)

[38] They had such a strong wind at the stern, that they reached Gaeta from Barcelona in five days and nights. They all had been thoroughly frightened because of the very rough weather. Throughout all that region, there was also fear of the plague, but as soon as he disembarked, he began the journey to Rome. Of those who came on the ship, a mother and her daughter whom she had dressed in boy's clothing,[1] and another youth, accompanied him. They joined him because they too were begging.

Having reached a lodge, they came upon a large bonfire with many soldiers around it. The soldiers gave them something to eat, and a good deal of wine, coaxing them as if they wanted to warm them up. Later they separated them, by placing the mother and daughter in a room upstairs, and the pilgrim and the youth in a stable. But at midnight, he heard loud cries coming from above. Getting up to see what it was, he found the mother and her daughter in the courtyard below, wailing and complaining that there was an attempt to rape them. At this, such a strong feeling came over him that he began to shout, "Must one put up with this?" and other similar protests. He uttered these words with such force that all those in the house were startled, and no one did him any harm. The youth had already fled. All three of them left that place, even though it was still night.

[39] When they arrived at a nearby city, they found it closed. Unable to enter, the three of them spent the night in a leaky church. In the morning, they were refused entry into the city, and they received no alms from anyone outside, even though they went to a castle that could be seen nearby. There, the pilgrim felt weak because of the hardships on the sea, and because of everything else, etc. Unable to travel further, he remained there. The mother and her daughter continued to Rome.

That day, many people left the city. Learning that the lady of the place was coming, he approached her. He told her that he was ill only from weakness, and asked her to let him enter the city to seek a cure. She readily granted this. He started to beg throughout the city, and obtained a fair amount. After two days of recovery there, he set out on his journey again, and arrived in Rome on Palm Sunday.

[40] Here, everyone who spoke to him, when they discovered that he did not carry any money for Jerusalem, tried to dissuade him from making the trip. They asserted with many arguments that it was impossible to obtain passage without money. Yet he had great assurance in his soul, and he could not doubt that he would find a way to go to Jerusalem. After receiving the blessing of Pope Adrian VI,[2] he set out for Venice eight or nine days after Easter. He did have six or seven ducats that someone had given him for the passage from Venice to Jerusalem. He accepted them because people had given him strong warnings that rattled him, namely that he would not be able to make the passage without it. Nevertheless, two days after leaving Rome, he began to realize that this was a lack of trust on his part. It bothered him greatly that he had accepted the ducats. He wondered if it would be good to get rid of them. Finally, he decided to give them spontaneously to anyone who approached him, who usually were beggars. As a result, when he finally arrived in Venice, he had only a small amount left, which he needed to spend for that night.

[41] On the journey to Venice, he slept in doorways because of the guards against the plague. It happened once, when he awakened in the morning, that he encountered a man who fled in horror after one look at him. Presumably, this was because he saw him so very pale. Traveling in this way, he came to Chioggia. There, he and some companions who had joined him learned that they were not allowed to enter Venice. His companions decided to continue to Padua to obtain a certificate of health there, so he set out with them. Yet he could not keep up with them, because they walked very fast. At nightfall, he found himself alone in a large field.

While he was there, Christ appeared to him in the manner in which he usually appeared to him, as we have mentioned above.[3] This brought him much comfort. Consoled thusly, the next morning, he chose not to forge a fake certificate of health, as I believe his companions had done. He came to the gates of Padua, and the guards let him enter without asking him anything. The same thing happened when he left. His companions were greatly astonished at this. They had just obtained a certificate to go to Venice, but he had not bothered about this.

[42] When they arrived at Venice, guards came to the boat to examine them all. They did so one by one, to as many passengers as were in it, but him alone they ignored. He supported himself in Venice by begging, and he slept in St. Mark's Square. Yet he never went to the house of the imperial ambassador,[4] nor did he take any special care to seek means for his passage. He had a great assurance in his soul that God would provide a way for him to go to Jerusalem. This gave him such confidence, that he could not doubt it, no matter the arguments or fears that people tried to give him.

One day, he bumped into a rich Spaniard who asked him what he was doing, and where he wanted to go. Learning his purpose, the man took him home to dinner, and kept him there for a few days, until everything was ready for the departure. Ever since Manresa, the pilgrim had the habit, whenever he ate with anyone, never to speak at table, except to answer briefly. Instead, he listened to what people were saying, and noted some things that he could use as opportunities to speak about God. When the meal was finished, he did so.[5]

[43] This was the reason why the worthy gentleman and all his household were so attached to him and wanted him to stay. They made an effort to keep him there. This same host brought him to the doge of Venice so that he could speak to him, which is to say, he obtained entrance and an audience for him. After the doge heard the

pilgrim speak, he ordered that someone give him passage on the ship of the government officials who were going to Cyprus.

Although many pilgrims to Jerusalem had arrived that year in Venice, most had returned home because of a recent event that had occurred, the capture of Rhodes. Even so, there were still thirteen on the pilgrim ship that sailed first, so that eight or nine remained to go on the government officials' ship.[6] As the ship was about to leave, our pilgrim had a severe bout of fever. It troubled him for a few days, but then left. The ship was sailing on a day when he had taken a purgative. The people of the house asked the doctor if the pilgrim could go to Jerusalem, and the doctor said that indeed he could, if he wanted to be buried there. But the pilgrim did embark and sail that day. He vomited so much that he felt greatly relieved, and he began to recover completely. There were some obscenities and indecencies openly practiced on the ship, which he condemned severely.[7]

[44] The Spaniards on the ship warned him not to do so, because the crew was planning to leave him on an island. Yet Our Lord deigned that they arrive quickly at Cyprus. Leaving the ship there, they went overland to another port called Las Salinas, ten leagues away. They boarded the pilgrim ship. Again, he brought no more for his sustenance than his hope in God, as he had done on the other ship.

During all that time, Our Lord appeared to him often, giving him great consolation and determination. What he seemed to see was something round and large, and as if made of gold. He began to see this after they left Cyprus and arrived at Jaffa.

They continued to Jerusalem on donkeys, as is usually done. Two miles before they reached Jerusalem, a Spaniard—a noble, it seemed, named Diego Manes—suggested to all the pilgrims with great devotion that, since they shortly would reach the place from which they could see the Holy City, it would be appropriate for all of them to prepare their consciences and go in silence.

[45] This seemed good to them all, and each began to recollect himself. A little before coming to the place from where they could see the city, they dismounted, because they saw the friars with the cross, awaiting them. Upon seeing the city, the pilgrim felt great consolation. Later, the others testified that they also had this reaction, with a joy that did not seem natural. He always felt this same devotion on his visits to the holy places.[8]

His firm resolution was to remain in Jerusalem, continually visiting those holy places. In addition to this devotion, he also had a resolution to help souls. For this purpose, he brought letters of recommendation for the guardian, and gave them to him.[9] He told him about his intention to remain there because of his devotion, but not about the second part about wanting to help souls, because he had not told this to anyone, while he had frequently made public the first.[10] The guardian answered that he did not see how he could stay, because the house was in such need that it could not even support the friars. For that reason, he had decided to send some of the friars with the pilgrims back to Europe. The pilgrim replied that he wanted nothing from the house, except that, if he visited sometimes to confess, they would hear his confession. Hearing that, the guardian told him that such an arrangement might work. But the pilgrim would have to wait for the arrival of the provincial, who was in Bethlehem at the time. I believe he was the head of the order in that area.

[46] With this promise, the pilgrim felt reassured. He began to write letters to Barcelona to spiritual persons.[11] Having already written one, and while writing another on the evening before the departure of the pilgrims, he received a summons from the provincial—for he had arrived—and from the guardian. The provincial spoke kindly to him, saying that he knew of his good intention to remain in those holy places. He said that he had given much thought to the matter, but because of his prior experiences with others, he judged that it was not expedient. For many pilgrims had the same desire, but some had been captured, and still others killed. Subsequently, the order had

been obliged to ransom the captives.[12] Therefore, he should prepare to leave the next day with the pilgrims.

To this, the pilgrim replied that he was very firm in his resolution, and that he was resolved to realize it under any circumstances. He gave them to understand quite bluntly that, even though the provincial thought otherwise, if there was nothing binding him under sin, he would not abandon his resolution because of any fears. To this, the provincial replied that they had authority from the Apostolic See to compel anyone to leave the place, or to remain there, as they saw fit; and likewise, to excommunicate anyone who was unwilling to obey them. The provincial went on to say that, in his particular case, they thought that he should not remain there, etc.

[47] The provincial wanted to show him the bulls giving them power to excommunicate, but he said he did not need to see them, as he believed their reverences. Given that they made this decision with the rightful authority that they had, he would obey them. When this was over, upon returning to his lodging, he felt a strong desire to visit Mount Olivet again before leaving, since it was not Our Lord's will that he remain in those holy places. On Mount Olivet, there is a stone from which Our Lord rose up to heaven, and his footprints are still visible there. This was what he wanted to see again.

So without saying anything or taking a guide—for those who go without a Turk as guide run a great risk—he slipped away from the others, and went alone to Mount Olivet. But the guards would not let him enter. He bribed them with a penknife that he carried. After praying with great consolation, he felt the desire to proceed to Bethphage. While there, he remembered that he had not noted on Mount Olivet on what side the right foot was, or on what side the left. Returning there, I think he gave his scissors to the guards so that they would let him enter.

[48] When the friars in the monastery discovered that he had gone like that without a guide, they took steps to find him. As he was coming down from Mount Olivet, he ran into a "belted" Christian who

served in the monastery.[13] He had a large staff, and with a great show of annoyance made as if to strike him. When he came up to the pilgrim, he grabbed him tightly by the arm, and the pilgrim readily let himself be led. The good man, however, never let him go. As the pilgrim went along this way, held thus by the belted Christian, he felt great consolation from Our Lord, so that it seemed to him that he saw Christ over him continually. The consolation continued intensely until he reached the monastery.

5. Return to Spain (October 1523 to February 1524)

[49] The next day, they set out. After arriving at Cyprus, the pilgrims dispersed in different ships. In the port, there were three or four ships bound for Venice. One was Turkish, another was a very small vessel, and the third was a very rich and powerful ship belonging to a wealthy Venetian. Some pilgrims asked the master of this ship to take the pilgrim. But when he learned that the pilgrim had no money, he was unwilling, even though many requested it, praising the pilgrim, etc.[1] The master answered that if he were such a saint, then he could make his passage as St. James had done, or something to that effect.[2] These same petitioners very easily succeeded with the master of the small vessel.

They set out one day with a good wind in the morning. In the afternoon, however, a storm came upon them, separating the ships one from the other. The big ship wrecked near those same islands of Cyprus, and only the passengers were saved. In the same storm, the Turkish ship sank, and all its passengers lost. The small vessel had great trouble, but in the end, they reached land somewhere in Apulia.

This was in the depth of winter, and it was very cold and snowing. The pilgrim had no clothing other than some breeches of coarse cloth—knee length and legs bare—with shoes and a doublet of black cloth, opened by many slashes at the shoulders, and a jacket that was short and quite thin.

[50] He arrived in Venice in mid-January of the year 1524. Starting in Cyprus, he had been at sea during the entire months of November and December, and what was gone of January. In Venice, one of the two who had welcomed him in their homes before he set out for Jerusalem, met him and gave him as alms fifteen or sixteen *giulii* and a piece of cloth, which he folded many times and put over his stomach because of the great cold.

After the pilgrim realized that it was not God's will that he stay in Jerusalem,[3] he continually pondered within himself *what ought to be done.*[4] Eventually, he became rather inclined to study for a while, so that he would be able to help souls.[5] He decided to go to Barcelona, so he left Venice for Genoa. One day, while praying his devotions in the principal church of Ferrara, a beggar asked him for alms, and he gave him a *marchetto*, which is a coin of five or six *quatrini*. After that, another beggar came, and he gave him another small coin that he had, somewhat larger. To a third, he gave a *giulio*, having nothing but *giulii*. The beggars kept coming, because they saw that he was giving alms, until all that he had was gone. Then a whole group of beggars came seeking alms. His response was to ask them pardon, as he had nothing left.

[51] He left Ferrara for Genoa. On the road, he met some Spanish soldiers who treated him well that night. They were greatly surprised that he traveled that road, because one had to pass practically between the two armies, the French and the imperial. They urged him to leave the highway, and to take a safer road that they showed him. He did not take their advice. Instead, traveling straight on, he came upon a burned and destroyed village. Thus, that night, he found no one to give him anything to eat. At sunset, he reached a walled place where the guards immediately seized him, thinking that he was a spy. They put him in a cabin next to the gate, and began to question him, as is usual when there is some suspicion. He replied to all their questions that he knew nothing. They stripped him and searched him down to his shoes, and all over his body, to see if he was carrying any letters. Unable to learn anything by any means, they seized him to bring him before the captain: "he would make him talk." The pilgrim asked them to let him cover himself with his jacket, but they refused to give it to him. They took him in the breeches and doublet mentioned above.

[52] On the way, the pilgrim had some sort of impression of when they led Christ away, but this was not a vision like the others. He was led down three large streets. He went without any sadness, but rather

with joy and satisfaction. It was his custom to address every person, no matter who it was, by using Vos, as he piously believed that Christ and the apostles had spoken in this way, etc.[6] As he was going in this way through the streets, it occurred to him that it would be wise to give up that custom in this situation, and to speak in a way that acknowledged the captain's authority. He thought this because of a fear of the tortures that they might inflict, etc. But he recognized that it was a temptation. "Since it is such," he said, "I will not acknowledge his authority, nor show him respect, nor take off my cap to him."

[53] They reached the captain's headquarters and left him in a lower room. A bit later, the captain spoke to him. Without using any form of courtesy, the pilgrim answered him curtly, and with a noticeable interval between one word and the next. The captain took him for a madman, and said so to those who had brought him. "This man is not in his senses. Give him his things and throw him out." Immediately upon leaving the headquarters, he met a Spaniard who lived there. He took him into his house and gave him something to break his fast, and all the necessities for that night.

Setting out in the morning, he traveled until evening. Two soldiers in a tower saw him and came down to seize him. They took him to their captain, who was French. The captain asked him, among other things, from what country he came. Learning that he was from Guipúzcoa, he said to him, "I come from near there," apparently from near Bayonne. Then he said, "Take him and give him supper and treat him well." On this road from Ferrara to Genoa, he had many other little experiences.

Finally, he reached Genoa, where a Biscayan named Portundo recognized him. He had met the pilgrim on other occasions when he served in the court of the Catholic king. This man got him passage on a ship to Barcelona. But the pilgrim came close to being captured by Andrea Doria, who had given chase to the ship, being then on the French side.[7]

6. Barcelona and Alcalá (February 1524 to June 1527)

[54] When he arrived at Barcelona, he made his inclination to study known to Isabella Roser and to a Master Ardévol who taught grammar.[1] To both, this seemed like a good idea. Ardévol offered to teach him for free, and she offered to give him what he needed to support himself. In Manresa, the pilgrim had known a friar—of the Order of St. Bernard, I think—a very spiritual man. He wanted to be with this friar in order to learn from him, and to be able to progress more rapidly in the spiritual life, and to be of help to souls. So the pilgrim replied that he would accept the offers of Roser and Ardévol if he did not find in Manresa all that he desired. When he went there, however, he learned that the friar was dead.

Returning to Barcelona, he began to study with great diligence. Yet something was hindering him greatly. Whenever he began to memorize, as one must in the beginnings of grammar, there came to him new insights into spiritual matters and new fascinations. They were so intense that he could not memorize, nor could he drive them away, no matter how much he resisted.

[55] So, thinking often about this, he said to himself, "Not even when I engage in prayer and am at Mass do such vivid insights come to me." Thus, little by little, he came to realize that it was a temptation.[2] After praying, he went to Our Lady of the Sea, near the master's house. The pilgrim had asked him please to listen to him just a little while in that church. When they both sat down, he told him exactly all that was happening in his soul, and what little progress he had made for that reason. The pilgrim promised this same master, saying, "I promise you that I will never fail to listen to you these two years, so long as I can find bread and water in Barcelona with which to support myself." Because he made this promise with great determination, he never again had those temptations.[3]

The stomach pain was gone that had afflicted him in Manresa, and for which reason he had worn shoes. He felt well in the stomach ever since he had embarked for Jerusalem. Thus, while he was studying in Barcelona, he desired to resume his previous penances. He cut holes in the soles of his shoes, which he kept widening little by little, so that by the time the winter cold came, he was wearing only the uppers.

[56] After two years of studying—during which time, people said that he had made great progress—his master informed him that he could now study the liberal arts, and that he should go to Alcalá. Nevertheless, he had a doctor of theology examine him, and he gave him the same advice. So he set out alone for Alcalá, although he already had some companions, I think.[4]

When he arrived at Alcalá, he began to beg and to live on alms. After he had lived in this fashion for ten or twelve days, a cleric and others who were with him, seeing him beg alms one day, began to laugh at him and to utter some insults, as one usually does to those who, being healthy, go begging.[5] At that moment, the superintendent of the new Hospice de Antezana passed by, and expressing regret at this, called to him, and took him to the hospice where he gave him a room and all that he needed.[6]

[57] He studied at Alcalá almost a year and a half. Since he had arrived in Barcelona in 1524, during Lent, and had studied there for two years, it was in 1526 that he reached Alcalá. He studied the logic of Soto, the physics of Albert, and the Master of the Sentences.[7] While at Alcalá, he was engaged in giving spiritual exercises and teaching Christian doctrine, and this bore fruit for the glory of God. There were many persons who came to a deep understanding and relish of spiritual things. But others had various temptations. There was one such who wanted to take the discipline but could not do so, as though the hand were held,[8] and other similar cases. These gave rise to talk among the people, especially because of the great crowd that gathered whenever he was explaining doctrine.[9]

Soon after he arrived at Alcalá, he became acquainted with Don Diego de Eguía, who was living with his brother, a wealthy printer in Alcalá.[10] They helped him with alms to give to the poor. The pilgrim's three companions lodged in his house. Once, when they came to ask alms for some needs, Don Diego said he had no money, but he opened for him a chest in which he had various objects. He gave him bed coverings of different colors, and candlesticks, and other such things. Wrapping them all in a sheet, the pilgrim put them on his shoulders and went off to aid the poor.

[58] As mentioned earlier, there was much talk throughout that region about the things happening at Alcalá. Some spoke one way about the companions, some spoke another. The matter reached the inquisitors at Toledo. When they came to Alcalá, the companions' host alerted the pilgrim, telling him that the inquisitors were calling them sack-wearers,[11] and, I believe, alumbrados,[12] and that they would crush them. The inquisitors began at once to investigate them, and to examine their life. Finally, they returned to Toledo without summoning them, because they had come solely for that purpose.

They left the trial to the vicar Figueroa, who is now with the emperor. A few days later, Figueroa summoned them and told them how an investigation and examination of their life had been made by the inquisitors, and that no error had been found in their teaching or in their life, and therefore they could continue as they were without any hindrance. Yet they were not members of a religious order, and so it did not seem appropriate for them to go about all in the same habit. It would be a good idea, and he ordered this, that two of them—he pointed to the pilgrim and to Arteaga[13]—dye their clothes black. The other two, Calisto[14] and Cáceres,[15] should dye theirs brown. "Little John," a French youth, could stay as he was.[16]

[59] The pilgrim says that they will do what they are ordered. "But," he says,

> I do not know what benefit these inquisitions bring. The other day a priest did not want to give the sacrament to someone

because he went to Communion every eight days. Priests were objecting to me, too.[17] We would like to know if the inquisitors found any heresy in us.

"No," says Figueroa, "for if they did, they would burn you." "They would burn you too," says the pilgrim, "if they found heresy in you." They dye their clothing as ordered. Fifteen or twenty days later, Figueroa orders the pilgrim not to go barefoot, but to wear shoes. So he complies without a fuss, as in all such matters in which he was ordered.[18]

Four months later, Figueroa himself began another investigation of them. Besides the usual reasons, I believe this was another factor, that a married woman of rank had special regard for the pilgrim. In order not to be noticed, she came to the hospice at dawn, wearing a veil, as is the custom in Alcalá de Henares. On entering, she removed her veil and went into the pilgrim's room.[19] But they did nothing to them this time either, nor did they say anything to them.[20]

[60] Four months later, he was living in a cabin just outside the hospice. One day, a bailiff came to his door and called him, saying, "Just come with me." He put him in jail and said to him, "You may not leave here until you are ordered otherwise." This was in the summer. Because he was not sequestered, many people came to visit him.[21]

He did the same things as when he was free, teaching and giving exercises. Never would he have an advocate or attorney, although many offered themselves. He especially remembers Doña Teresa de Cárdenas, who sent someone to visit him, and who frequently offered to get him out. But he accepted nothing, always answering, "He for whose love I got in here will get me out, if he is served thereby."

[61] He was in prison seventeen days without being examined or knowing the reason for it. At the end of that time, Figueroa came to the jail and examined him about many things, even including whether he taught people to keep the Sabbath.[22] He asked whether he knew two particular women, a mother and her daughter. To

this, he said yes. Then he asked whether he had known about their departure before they left. To this, he said no, under the oath that he had taken. The vicar then placed a hand on his shoulder, and with a happy expression on his face, said, "This is the reason why you were brought here."

Among the pilgrim's many devotees were a mother and her daughter, both widowed. The daughter was very young and attractive. They had made great spiritual progress, especially the daughter. So much so, that although they were noblewomen, they had gone to the Veronica of Jaén on foot, by themselves, and apparently begging.[23] This caused considerable gossip in Alcalá. Doctor Ciruelo, who was somewhat responsible for them, thought that the prisoner had persuaded them to do this, and for this reason, he had him arrested.[24]

Having heard the vicar's words, the prisoner said to him, "Would you like me to speak more at length about this affair?" He said, "Yes." "Then you should know," said the prisoner,

> that these two women have often insisted with me that they wanted to go about the world serving the poor in one hospice or another.[25] I always dissuaded them from this resolution, because the daughter is so young and attractive, etc. I told them that if they wanted to visit the poor, they could do it in Alcalá, and they could accompany the Blessed Sacrament.

When this conversation was finished, Figueroa left with his notary, taking a complete written statement.

[62] At that time, Calisto was in Segovia. Learning of the pilgrim's imprisonment, he came at once, although he had only recovered from a serious illness, and joined him in the jail. But Calisto for his part suggested that it would be better to report the situation to the vicar general. The latter received him kindly, but indicated that he would have to send him back to the jail, because that is where he needed to be until those women returned, to see if they could confirm what

Calisto had said. Calisto remained in jail a few days, but when the pilgrim saw that this harmed his physical health, because he was not yet entirely well, he had him released with the help of a doctor, a great friend of his.

Forty-two days passed from the day the pilgrim entered jail until they set him free. Near the end of that incarceration, after the two pious women returned, the notary came to the jail to read the sentence. He could go free. But the companions should dress like other students, and should not speak about matters of faith, until they had studied for four more years, because they had no education. For in truth, the pilgrim was the one who had the most education, and that was with little foundation. This was the first thing he used to say whenever they examined him.[26]

[63] Because of this sentence, he was somewhat doubtful about what he should do. They seemed to be shutting down his ministry of helping souls, but without giving him any other reason than he had not studied. Finally, he decided to go to Fonseca, the archbishop of Toledo, to put the case in his hands.[27] He set out from Alcalá and found the archbishop in Valladolid. Faithfully recounting the affair to him, he said that, even though he was not now in his jurisdiction, nor obliged to abide by the sentence, he would still do what he commanded in this matter. He addressed him as Vos, as was his custom with everyone.[28] The archbishop received him very well, adding that he had friends and a college at Salamanca too. He put all of this at the pilgrim's disposal. Just as the archbishop was leaving, he had four escudos given to him.

7. Trouble at Salamanca (July to December 1527)

[64] On his arrival in Salamanca, while he was praying in a church, he was recognized by a devoted friend of the group, for his four companions had been there some days already. She asked him his name, and then took him to the lodgings of his companions.

When the sentence had been given in Alcalá that they should dress like students, the pilgrim said, "When you ordered us to dye our clothes, we did so. But now we cannot comply because we do not have the means to buy them." So the vicar general himself provided them with clothing and caps and all the other student gear. Dressed in this fashion, they had left Alcalá.

At Salamanca, he went to confession to a Dominican friar at St. Stephen's. Ten or twelve days after his arrival, the confessor said to him one day, "The fathers of the house would like to speak with you." And he replied, "In the name of God." "Then," said the confessor, "it would be well if you came here to dine on Sunday. But I warn you about something: they will want to know many things from you."

So on Sunday he came with Calisto. After dinner, the subprior, in the absence of the prior, together with the confessor and, I think, another friar, went with them to a chapel. With great geniality, the subprior began to speak of the good reports that they had heard about their life and ways, and that they went about preaching in apostolic fashion. They would be pleased to learn about these things in greater detail. The subprior began by asking what they had studied. The pilgrim replied, "Of all of us, I am the one who has studied the most," and he gave a clear account of the little he had studied, and with what little foundation.

[65] "Well, then, what do you preach?" "We do not preach," said the pilgrim, "but we do speak familiarly with some people about the things of God. For example, after dinner, with some people who invite us." "But," said the friar, "what things of God do you speak about? That is just what we would like to know." "We speak," said the

pilgrim, "sometimes of one virtue, sometimes of another, always in praise of it. Or we speak of one vice or another, always condemning it." "You are not learned men," said the friar, "and you speak about virtues and vices. But no one can speak about these except in one of two ways: either through learning or through the Holy Spirit. If it's not through learning, then through the Holy Spirit."[1]

At this, the pilgrim was somewhat on his guard, because that kind of argument did not seem good to him. After being silent a while, he said it was not necessary to speak further of these matters. The friar insisted, "Well, now that there are so many errors of Erasmus and of so many others who have deceived the world, you do not wish to explain what you say?"[2]

[66] The pilgrim said, "Father, I will say no more than what I already have, unless it is before my superiors who can oblige me to do so."

Before this, the friar had asked why Calisto came dressed as he was. He wore a short tunic and a large hat on his head, with a staff in his hand, and boots almost halfway up the leg. Because he was very tall, he looked rather ridiculous. The pilgrim related how they had been imprisoned in Alcalá, and how they had been ordered to dress like students, and how his companion Calisto, because of the great heat, had given his gown to a poor cleric. At this, the friar seemed to mutter to himself, "Charity begins at home," indicating that he was not pleased.

Well, getting back to the story: the subprior, unable to get any other word out of the pilgrim but that, said, "Then remain here, and we will indeed make you tell everything." Then all the friars left in haste. Before that, the pilgrim had asked if they wanted them to remain in that chapel, or where they wanted them to wait. The subprior answered that they should remain in the chapel. The friars then closed all the doors and, apparently, took up the matter with the judges. The two of them were in the monastery for three days, eating in the refectory with the friars, without anyone saying something to them in the name of the court. Their room was usually full of friars who came to see them. The pilgrim always spoke on his usual topics. As a result, there was already some division among the friars, many showing that they were sympathetic.

[67] At the end of three days, a notary came and took them to jail. They were not put down below, with the criminals, but in an upper room that was very dirty, because it was old and unused. They were both bound with the same chain, each one by his foot.[3] The chain was attached to a post in the middle of the house, and would have been about five or six feet long. Each time that one of them wanted to do something, the other had to accompany him. All that night they stayed awake. The next day, when their imprisonment was known in the city, people sent to the jail something on which they could sleep, and all that was needed, in abundance. And always there was a crowd to visit them, and the pilgrim kept up his practice of speaking about God, etc.

The bachelor Frias came to examine each of them separately. The pilgrim gave him all his papers to be examined, which were the *Exercises*. When asked if they had companions, they said that they did, and indicated where they were. Straightaway some went there, on the bachelor's orders, and brought Cáceres and Arteaga to the jail. But they left Little John, who later became a friar. However, they did not put them above with the other two, but down where the common prisoners were. Like before, he refused to have an advocate or attorney.

[68] Some days later, he was summoned before four judges: the three doctors, Sanctisidoro, Paravinhas, and Frias; and the fourth was the bachelor Frias. All of them had already seen the Exercises. Now they asked him many things, not only about the Exercises but also about theology. For example, they asked about the Trinity and the Eucharist, and how he understood these articles. First he began speaking in his normal way.[4] But then, after being ordered by the judges, he spoke in such a manner that they had no reason to fault him. The bachelor Frias, who during this process had taken a more prominent role, also

asked him about a canonical case. He was required to answer everything, but he always said first that he did not know what scholars said about those matters.

Then they ordered him to explain the first commandment in the way he usually explained it. He started to do so, and he took so long, and said so many things about the first commandment, that they were not inclined to ask him more. Before this, when they were speaking about the *Exercises*, they insisted a good deal on one particular point, which was at the beginning: when entertaining a bad thought is a mortal sin, or only a venial sin. Their question was how he, without studies, could make that kind of determination. He answered, "Decide for yourselves whether what I say is true. If it is not, then condemn it."[5] But in the end, they left without condemning anything.

[69] Among the many who came to speak to him in jail, one was Don Francisco de Mendoza, who now has the title of cardinal of Burgos. He came with the bachelor Frias. In a friendly way, he asked how he was doing in prison, and if it bothered him to be imprisoned. He replied,

> I will answer what I answered today to a lady who, on seeing me in prison, spoke words of compassion. I said to her, "By this you show that you do not wish to be imprisoned for the love of God. Does imprisonment seem to be such a great evil to you? Well, I will tell you that there are not so many fetters and chains in Salamanca, that I do not want more for the love of God."[6]

About this time, it happened that all the prisoners in the jail fled. But the two companions who were with them did not flee. In the morning, they were found there alone, with the doors open, and without anyone guarding them.[7] Everyone was deeply edified. There was much talk in the city, and they gave them an entire mansion that was nearby, as a prison.

[70] After twenty-two days of imprisonment, they were summoned to hear the sentence, which was that no error was found in their life or teaching. Therefore they could do what they had been doing, teaching doctrine and speaking about the things of God, provided that they did not define for people whether this particular sin is mortal or venial, until they had spent four more years in studies. After the sentence was read, the judges displayed great affection, apparently wishing to give the impression that they were being generous. The pilgrim said that he would do everything the sentence required, but he did not think that it was acceptable, because without condemning him for anything, they shut his mouth in such a way that he could not help people to his full ability. But as much as Doctor Frias urged him, and showed himself very well disposed to him, the pilgrim said nothing more, except that, as long as he were within the jurisdiction of Salamanca, he would do what they had ordered.

Then they were released from jail. He began to commend the matter to God, and to think about what he ought to do. He found great difficulty in remaining in Salamanca, for it seemed to him that his ministry of helping souls had been shut down by this prohibition not to define mortal and venial sin.

[71] So he decided to go to Paris to study.[8] When the pilgrim was considering in Barcelona whether he should study and how much, his one concern had been whether, after he had studied, he would enter a religious institute or go about the world. When thoughts of entering an institute came to him, then he also had the desire to enter a decadent and not quite reformed one—if he were to be a member of a religious order—so that he would suffer more in it, in which case, he thought that God would help them. And God gave him great confidence that he would endure easily all the insults and injuries they might inflict.[9]

Now, at the time of his imprisonment in Salamanca, he still felt the same desire that he always had, to help souls. For that reason, he decided to study. He also decided to recruit others with the same resolution, while also taking steps to keep the companions whom he already had.[10] Determined to go to Paris, he arranged with these companions that they would wait there, while he went to see if he could gather the resources for their studies.[11]

[72] Many important persons urged him strongly not to go. But they could never dissuade him. On the contrary, fifteen or twenty days after leaving prison, he set out alone, riding a donkey, and taking some books. When he arrived at Barcelona, all those who knew him advised him against the journey to France, because of the fierce wars. They recounted very specific incidents, even telling him that they had put Spaniards on spits. But he never had any kind of fear.

8. Progress in Paris (February 1528 to April 1535)

[73] So he set out for Paris, alone and on foot. He reached Paris in the month of February, or thereabouts. And as he tells me, this was in the year 1528 or 1527.[1] He lodged in a house with some Spaniards, and went to study humanities at Montaigu.[2] The reason was that, as they had made him advance with such haste in studies, he found himself very deficient in fundamentals. He studied with young boys, following the order and method of Paris.[3]

When he first arrived in Paris, a merchant gave him twenty-five *escudos* on a draft from Barcelona. The pilgrim gave these to one of the Spaniards in those lodgings for safekeeping. But in a short time, the Spaniard had spent them, and he did not have the means to pay him back. So already at the end of Lent, the pilgrim had nothing left of the *escudos*, both because of his own expenses, and because of the reason mentioned above. He was compelled to beg, and even to leave the house where he was staying.

[74] The hospice of St. James, past the Church of the Holy Innocents, took him in. The hospice was a good distance from the college of Montaigu, which greatly inconvenienced him in his studies. In order to find the hospice door unlocked, one had to return at the sound of the Angelus, and to leave in daylight. Thus he could not attend his lectures properly. Having to beg alms to support himself was another obstacle.

He began to subject himself to greater penances and fasts, because it was almost five years now that he felt no stomach pains. After some time in this life of hospice and begging, he saw that he was making little progress in studies. So he began to consider what he should do. As there were several students who served some of the regents in the colleges, and had time to study, he decided to seek a master.[4]

[75] He found great consolation in the following reflection and resolution that he entertained: he imagined that the master would be Christ, and that he would call one of the students "St. Peter," and

another "St. John," and so with each one of the apostles. "When the master orders me, I will think that Christ orders me. When another orders me, I will think that St. Peter orders me."

He tried hard to find a master. He spoke to the bachelor Castro,[5] and also to a Carthusian friar who knew many teachers, and to others. None could find him a master.

[76] As he found no solution, at last a Spanish friar told him one day that it would be better for him to go each year to Flanders. He could spend two months there, or even less, to secure the means to study for the whole year. After commending this to God, it seemed like a good idea to him. Following this advice, each year he brought back from Flanders enough funds to sustain himself in one way or another. Once, he also went to England, and collected more alms than he usually did in other years.

[77] The first time he returned from Flanders, he got more involved than usual in spiritual conversations, and he gave exercises almost simultaneously to three persons, namely Peralta,[6] the bachelor Castro who was at the Sorbonne, and a Biscayan named Amador,[7] who was at St. Barbara. They were quite transformed, so that they gave all they had to the poor, even their books, and began to beg alms through Paris. They went to lodge in the hospice of St. James, where the pilgrim had stayed before. But by that time he had left there, for the reasons mentioned above.

This caused great commotion in the university, because the first two men were distinguished and well known. The Spaniards then began a campaign against the two masters. Because they were not able to convince them to return to the university with much argument and persuasion, they instead went armed one day to the hospice and dragged them out.

[78] When they were brought to the university, an agreement was made. After they had finished their studies, then could carry out

their resolutions. The bachelor Castro later went to Spain, where he preached at Burgos for some time, and then became a Carthusian friar in Valencia.[8] Peralta set out on foot as a pilgrim to Jerusalem. In these circumstances, a captain who was a relative of his captured him in Italy. He made efforts to bring him to the pope, who ordered Peralta to return to Spain. These things did not happen immediately, but some years later.

Great complaints arose in Paris, especially among the Spaniards, about the pilgrim. Master Gouvea was saying that he had caused Amador, who was in his college, to go mad. Gouvea had determined, and said so aloud, that he would subject the pilgrim to a formal beating as a seducer of students, the first time that he showed up at St. Barbara.

[79] The Spaniard with whom he had stayed at the beginning, and who had spent his money without paying it back, left for Spain by way of Rouen. He fell sick while awaiting passage there. While he was ill, the pilgrim learned of it from a letter that he had sent, and felt a desire to visit him and to help him. He also thought that, in those circumstances, he could win him over to leave the world and give himself completely to the service of God.[9]

In order to achieve this, he felt the desire to walk the twenty-eight leagues from Paris to Rouen barefoot, without eating or drinking. As he prayed over this, he felt very afraid. Finally, he went to the monastery of St. Dominic, and there he decided to go in the manner just mentioned. The great fear that he had of tempting God had passed.[10]

He got up early the next day, the morning that he was going to leave. As he began to dress, such a great fear came over him that he seemed almost unable to dress himself. Despite that repugnance, he left the house, and the city too, shortly before dawn. Still the fear was with him constantly, and it persisted as far as Argenteuil, which is a walled town three leagues from Paris on the way to Rouen, where the garment of Our Lord is said to be. He passed the town in that spiritual distress, but as he climbed a small hill, that feeling began to leave him.

He felt great consolation and spiritual strength, and with such joy that he began to shout through the fields and to speak to God, etc.

He lodged that evening with a poor beggar in a hospice, having traveled fourteen leagues that day. The next day, he sought shelter in a barn. On the third day, he reached Rouen. All this time, he went without eating or drinking, and barefoot, as he had determined. In Rouen, he consoled the sick man, and helped him board a ship for Spain. He also gave him letters directing him to the companions who were in Salamanca, namely Calisto, Cáceres, and Arteaga.

[80] Not to have to speak further of these companions, their fate was this.[11] While the pilgrim was in Paris, he wrote frequently to them, as they had agreed. He wrote about the scant facilities he had to bring them to Paris to study. Nevertheless, he had undertaken to write to Doña Leonor de Mascarenhas,[12] that she might assist Calisto by writing letters to the court of the king of Portugal, requesting that Calisto obtain one of the scholarships that the king of Portugal gave [to Portuguese students studying] in Paris. Doña Leonor gave Calisto the letters, and a mule to ride, and money for his expenses. Calisto went to the court of the king of Portugal, but in the end, he did not go to Paris. Instead, after returning to Spain, he went to the Imperial Indies with a certain spiritual woman. He returned to Spain later, but went to the same Indies once more, and this time returned to Spain a rich man. He thus surprised all in Salamanca who had known him before.[13]

Cáceres returned to Segovia, which was his hometown. There he began to live in such a manner that he seemed to have forgotten his first resolution.[14]

Arteaga was made a *comendador*.[15] Later, when the Society was established in Rome, he was offered a bishopric in the Indies. He wrote to the pilgrim, asking that he give it to a member of the Society, but the request was refused. So he went to the Imperial Indies as a bishop, and died there in strange circumstances. He happened to be ill, and there were two bottles there for his recovery. One had water, which the doctor had ordered for him. The other had Water of Soliman, a poison. The latter was given to him by mistake, and it killed him.[16]

[81] The pilgrim returned to Paris from Rouen. He discovered that because of the affair of Castro and Peralta there was much talk about him, and that the inquisitor had issued a summons for him. Without any delay, he went to the inquisitor, and said to him that he understood he was looking for him. He further said that he was prepared for anything he might want—the inquisitor was our Master Ory, a Dominican friar[17]—but he would request that he expedite it, because he wanted to enroll in the arts course on the coming feast of St. Remigius. He wanted to get this business over first, so that he could focus better on his studies. But the inquisitor did not summon him further. He only said that it was true that people had spoken of his doings, etc.

[82] A short time after this came St. Remy's, that is, the first of October, and he enrolled in the arts course under a teacher named Master Juan Peña. He enrolled with the resolution of retaining those companions who had the same resolution to serve the Lord, but not to go in search of others,[18] so that he could study more earnestly.

When he began to attend the lectures of the course, the same temptations came to him as when he was studying grammar in Barcelona. Whenever he was at a lecture, he could not pay attention because of the many spiritual thoughts that came to him. Realizing that in this way he made little progress in study, he went to his master, and promised him that he would never fail to follow the whole course, so long as he could find bread and water for his sustenance. After making this promise, all that devotion that came to him at an inappropriate time left him, and he went on quietly with his studies.

At this time, he associated with Master Peter Faber and Master Francis Xavier, both of whom he later won for God's service by means of the Exercises.[19]

At that stage in his course, university authorities did not harass him like before. On the subject of that resolution [to recruit companions], Doctor Frago once remarked to him how he marveled that the pilgrim went about so peacefully, without anyone giving him trouble. He replied, "The reason is that I do not speak to anyone of the things of God. But once the course is over, we'll be back to business as usual."

[83] While the two of them were speaking, a friar approached Doctor Frago to ask him to help find him a house, because in the one where he was lodging, many people had died. He thought it was because of the plague, which was then beginning in Paris. Doctor Frago and the pilgrim wished to see the house. They took a woman who was well versed in these matters. Upon entering, she confirmed that it was the plague. The pilgrim also chose to enter. Coming upon a sick person, he comforted him and touched his sore with his hand. After he had comforted and encouraged him a while, he went off alone. His hand began to hurt, so that it seemed to him that he had caught the plague. This impression was so strong that he could not overcome it, until he thrust his hand forcefully into his mouth, and moved it about inside, saying, "If you have the plague in the hand, then you will also have it in the mouth." When he had done this, he was rid of the impression, and of the pain in the hand.[20]

[84] But when he returned to the college of St. Barbara where he had been lodging and was attending the course, those in the college who knew that he had entered the plague-ridden house fled from him and would not let him enter. So he was forced to remain outside for several days.

It is the custom in Paris for those who are studying arts in the third year, in order to receive the baccalaureate, "to take a stone," as they say.[21] And because that costs an *escudo*, those who are very poor cannot do it. The pilgrim began to wonder whether it would be good for him to take it. Finding himself in great doubt, and undecided, he determined to put the matter in the hands of his master, who advised him to take it. And so he did. But critics were not lacking. Or at least, there was one Spaniard who made a malicious comment.

At this time, in Paris, he was quite sick in his stomach, so that every fifteen days he had a stomachache that lasted over an hour, and gave him a fever. Once, the stomachache lasted sixteen or seventeen hours. By this time, he had already finished the arts course, and had studied theology for some years, and had recruited the companions.[22] His trouble kept getting worse and worse. He could not find a cure, although many were tried.

[85] The doctors said that no other means were left to cure him, except to return to his native air. The companions gave him the same advice, and pressed him hard on the matter. Already by this time, they had all determined what they would do, namely go to Venice and to Jerusalem and spend their lives for the good of souls.[23] And if they were not given permission to remain in Jerusalem, then they would return to Rome and present themselves to the vicar of Christ, so that he could make use of them wherever he thought it would be more for the glory of God and the good of souls.[24] They also planned to wait a year in Venice for passage. If no passage to the East was available for them within a year, then they would be free of their vow about Jerusalem, and they would approach the pope, etc.

In the end, the pilgrim let himself be persuaded by the companions. The Spaniards among them also had some business that he could settle.[25] They agreed that when he felt well, he should go and attend to their business, and then proceed to Venice, where he would wait for the companions.

[86] This was in the year 1535. According to their agreement, the other companions were to depart [Paris for Venice] in 1537, on January 25, the feast of the conversion of St. Paul. In fact, however, because of the outbreak of war, they left earlier, in November of 1536.

As the pilgrim was about to leave, he learned that someone had brought a case against him to the inquisitor. Being aware of this, but seeing that they did not summon him, he went to the inquisitor and told him what he had heard. He told him that he was about to leave for Spain, and that he had some companions. So would he please pass a sentence? The inquisitor said it was true there was an accusation, but he did not find anything of importance in it. He only wanted to see the pilgrim's manuscript of the *Exercises*. When he saw it, he praised it very much, and asked the pilgrim to let him have the copy, which he did. Nevertheless, the pilgrim again insisted that they close his case with a formal sentence.[26] As the inquisitor was making excuses, the pilgrim brought a public notary and witnesses to the inquisitor's house, and obtained formal testimony on this whole affair.

9. Farewell to Spain (October to November 1535)

[87] With that done, he mounted the pony the companions had bought for him, and he set out toward home alone. Along the way, he felt much better. When he arrived in the province,[1] he left the highway and took the mountain road, which was more secluded. Having proceeded a bit, he saw two armed men who were approaching him. That road is somewhat notorious for assassins. Shortly after they passed him, they turned around and approached him in great haste. He was a little afraid. All the same, he spoke to them, and learned that they were servants of his brother, who had sent them to meet him. Apparently, the brother had received news of the pilgrim's coming from Bayonne in France, where the pilgrim had been recognized. So the two men went ahead of him, and he continued on the same road.

Just before he reached home, he came upon the aforementioned men, who were approaching him again. They were very insistent about taking him to his brother's house, but they could not constrain him.[2] So he went to the hospice, and later, at a convenient hour, he went to seek alms in the area.

[88] In this hospice, he began to speak with many visitors about the things of God, by whose grace much fruit was derived. As soon as he had arrived, he decided to teach Christian doctrine every day to children, but his brother strongly objected to this, saying that no one would come.[3] He replied that one would be enough. But after he began to do it, many came repeatedly to hear him, even his brother.

Besides Christian doctrine, he also preached on Sundays and feasts, with profit and help to the souls who came many miles to hear him. He also made an attempt to eliminate some abuses, and with God's help some were corrected. For example, he persuaded the one administering justice to have gambling banned under sanction. There was also another abuse there. Girls in that region traditionally go about with their heads uncovered, and they do not cover them until they are married. But many have become partners of priests and other men, and are as faithful to them as though they were their wives. This is so common that the partners are not at all ashamed to say that they have their heads covered for so-and-so, and they are acknowledged as such.

[89] Much evil results from this custom. The pilgrim persuaded the governor to make a law that all those who covered the head for any-one, and who were not the wives, should be legally punished. And so this abuse began to be corrected. He arranged that the city provide for the poor on a regular basis, and that the city bells should be rung three times at the Angelus, that is, morning, noon, and evening, so that the people might pray as they do in Rome.

He felt well at the beginning but later fell seriously ill. Once he recovered, he decided to set out to attend to the affairs that his com-panions had entrusted to them, and to make the trip without money. At this, his brother was very upset, and ashamed that he should go on foot. By evening, the pilgrim was willing to make this compromise: to go on horseback with his brother and other relatives to the border of the province.

[90] But when he left the province, he dismounted and proceeded without taking anything. He went to Pamplona, and from there to Almazán, Father Laínez's home. Then he went to Sigüenza and Toledo, and from Toledo to Valencia. In all these birthplaces of his companions, he would not take anything, although the people offered him many things with great insistence.

In Valencia, he spoke with Castro who was a Carthusian monk.[4] He wanted to sail to Genoa, but good friends in Valencia begged him not to do so, because Barbarossa was on the sea with many ships, etc. Although they did say many things, enough to frighten him, never-theless nothing made him hesitate.

[91] Boarding a large ship, he passed through the storm mentioned above, when it was said that he was on the point of death three times.

When he arrived at Genoa, he took the road to Bologna, on which he had many difficulties. On one particular occasion, he lost his way. He began to walk parallel to a river that was down below, while the road he was taking was high above. The farther he went, the narrower the road became. Eventually it became so narrow that he could no longer go forward nor turn back. So he began to crawl. In this way, he covered a long distance in great fear, because each time he moved, he thought that he would fall into the river. It was the greatest physical stress that he had ever experienced, but finally he made it.

On his way into Bologna, while crossing over a wooden foot-bridge, he fell off. When he got up, covered with mud and water, he made many onlookers laugh. Entering Bologna, he began to beg alms, but he did not get one small coin, even though he tried every-where. He was ill for some time in Bologna, but afterward he went on to Venice, always in the same manner.

10. Venice and Vicenza (January 1536 to October 1537)

[92] During that time in Venice, he busied himself giving the Spiritual Exercises, and engaging in other spiritual conversations. The most distinguished persons to whom he gave the Exercises were Master Pietro Contarini and Master Gaspar de Doctis, and a Spaniard whose name was Rozas.

There was also another Spaniard there called the bachelor Hoces, who was in close touch with the pilgrim, and also with the bishop of Cette.[1] Although Hoces had some desire to make the Exercises, still he did not put it into execution. At last, he decided to begin making them. And having made them for three or four days, he spoke his mind to the pilgrim, telling him that because of the things someone had told him, he had been afraid that he would be taught some evil doctrine in the Exercises. For this reason, he had brought with him certain books, so he could have recourse to them, if perchance the pilgrim tried to deceive him. The Exercises helped him very much, and in the end, he resolved to imitate the pilgrim's life. He was also the first [of the pilgrim's companions] to die.

[93] In Venice, the pilgrim also endured another persecution, with many saying that his effigy had been burned in Spain and in Paris. This business went so far that a trial was held, and sentence was given in favor of the pilgrim.

The nine companions came to Venice at the beginning of 1537.[2] There they separated to serve in various hospices. After two or three months, they all went to Rome to obtain the blessing for the journey to Jerusalem. The pilgrim did not go, because of Doctor Ortiz, and also because of the new Theatine cardinal. The companions returned from Rome with drafts for two hundred or three hundred *escudos*, which had been given to them as alms for the journey to Jerusalem. They did not want to take anything except in drafts. Later, not being able to go to Jerusalem, they gave them back to the donors.

The companions returned to Venice in the fashion they had gone, that is, on foot and begging. They divided themselves into three groups, and in such a way that they were always of different nationalities.[3] There in Venice, those who were not ordained were ordained priests,[4] and the nuncio who was then in Venice—and who was later known as Cardinal Verallo—gave them faculties. They were ordained *ad titulum paupertatis* and all made vows of chastity and poverty.[5]

[94] In that year, no ships sailed for the East, because the Venetians had broken with the Turks. So, seeing that their hope of sailing was postponed, they dispersed within the Venetian region, with the intention of waiting until the year they had decided upon. If it expired without the possibility of travel [to Jerusalem], they would go to Rome.

It fell to the pilgrim to go with Faber and Laínez to Vicenza. There they found a certain house outside the city, which had neither doors nor windows. They stayed in it, sleeping on a little straw that they had brought. Twice a day, two of them always left to seek alms in the city, but they got so little that they could hardly sustain themselves. They usually ate a little toasted bread when they had it, and the one who remained at home took care of the toasting. In this way, they spent forty days, not doing anything other than prayer.

[95] After forty days, Master Jean Codure arrived. The four of them together decided to begin preaching. The four went to different piazzas, and began to preach on the same day, and at the same hour, by first shouting loudly and waving at people with their caps. Their preaching caused a great stir in the city. Many persons were moved with devotion, and the four received more material goods than they needed.

During the time he was at Vicenza, he had many spiritual visions, and many quite regular consolations, which was the contrary of what he experienced in Paris. In all that traveling, he had great supernatural experiences like those he used to have when he was in Manresa,[6] especially when he began to prepare for the priesthood in Venice, and when he was preparing to say Mass.

While he was still in Vicenza, he learned that one of the companions, who was at Bassano, was ill to the point of death.[7] At the same time, he too was ill with fever. Nevertheless, he set out and walked so vigorously that Faber, his companion, could not keep up with him. On that journey, he had assurance from God, and he told Faber so, that the companion would not die of that illness. On their arriving at Bassano, the sick man was much comforted and soon recovered. Then they all returned to Vicenza. All ten of them were there for some time. Some of them used to seek alms in the towns around Vicenza.

[96] Then, the year having passed with no passage made available, they decided to go to Rome. Even the pilgrim went, because on the earlier occasion when the other companions had gone without him, two churchmen about whom he had doubts had shown themselves very kind. The companions went to Rome divided into three or four groups, the pilgrim with Faber and Laínez.

On this journey, God visited him in a very special way. After he became a priest, he decided to wait a year without saying Mass, in order to prepare himself, and praying to Our Lady that she deign to place him with her Son.[8] One day, a few miles before reaching Rome, he was at prayer in a church, and he experienced such a change in his soul, and saw so clearly that God the Father had placed him with Christ his Son, that he would not dare to doubt it. God the Father had placed him with his Son.[9]

[97] When they arrived in Rome, he told the companions that he saw the windows were closed, by which he meant that they would face much hostile interference from others.

He also said, "We must be very much on our guard, and not have contacts with women, unless they are prominent." With regard to this resolution, sometime later, in Rome, Master Francis was confessor to a woman, and he sometimes visited her to speak of spiritual matters. She was subsequently found to be pregnant, but the Lord deigned that the one who had done the mischief should be discovered. The same kind of thing happened to Jean Codure, with a spiritual daughter of his who was caught with a man.

11. Finally in Rome (November 1537 to October 1538)

[98] From Rome, the pilgrim went to Monte Cassino to give the Exercises to Doctor Ortiz. He was there forty days, and on one of them, he had a vision of the bachelor Hoces entering heaven.[1] This brought him many tears and great spiritual consolation. He saw this so clearly, that if he said the contrary, he would feel like he was lying. From Monte Cassino, he brought with him Francis de Strada, and returning to Rome, he busied himself helping souls. They were still living at the vineyard. He gave the Spiritual Exercises to various people at the same time, one of whom lived at Saint Mary Major, the other at Ponte Sesto.

Then the persecutions began. Miguel began to give trouble and to speak badly of the pilgrim, who caused him to be summoned before the governor.[2] He first showed the governor a letter written by Miguel in which he praised the pilgrim very much.[3] The governor examined Miguel, and ended by banishing him from Rome.

Mudarra and Barreda then began their persecution, saying that the pilgrim and his companions were fugitives from Spain, from Paris, and from Venice. In the end, both of them confessed in the presence of the governor and the legate, who was then in Rome, that they had nothing bad to say about them, neither regarding their ways nor regarding their teaching. The legate ordered silence to be imposed on the whole affair, but the pilgrim did not accept that, saying he wanted a definite sentence.[4] This did not please the legate nor the governor nor even those who at first favored the pilgrim. But at last, after some months, the pope came to Rome. The pilgrim went to speak to him at Frascati, and informed him of several reasons for the investigations against him.[5] Thus informed, the pope ordered the sentence to be given, and it was given in his favor, etc.

With the help of the pilgrim and his companions, some pious works such as the Catechumens, Saint Martha, the Orphans, etc., were begun in Rome.

Master Nadal can recount the rest.[6]

Epilogue of Fr. Gonçalves

[99] After these things had been recounted, I asked the pilgrim on October 20 about the Exercises and the Constitutions, because I wanted to know how he had written them. He told me that he had not composed the Exercises all at once. When he noticed some things in his soul and found them useful, he thought that they might also be useful to others also, and so he put them in writing, such as the examination of conscience with that arrangement of lines, etc.[1] He told me that he had derived the elections in particular[2] from that diversity of spirits and thoughts that he had at Loyola, when he was still suffering in the leg. He told me that he would speak to me about the Constitutions in the evening.

The same day, he summoned me before supper, and with the air of a person who was more recollected than usual, he made a sort of protestation to me, the sum of which was to indicate the pure intention and sincerity with which he had related these things.[3] He said he was quite sure he had not exaggerated, and although he had committed many offenses against Our Lord after he began to serve him, that he had never consented to mortal sin. Rather, he had always grown in devotion, that is, ease in finding God, and now more than ever in his whole life. Every time, at any hour, that he wished to find God, he found him. Even now, he often had visions, especially of the kind mentioned earlier, when he saw Christ as the sun. This often happened while he was engaged in important matters, and that gave him confirmation.

[100] He also had many visions when he said Mass, and when he was drawing up the Constitutions too, he had them very often. He can now affirm this more easily, because every day he wrote down what went on in his soul, and he had it now in writing.[4] He showed me a rather large bundle of writings, of which he read to me a good bit.

Most were visions that he saw in confirmation of some aspect of the *Constitutions*, at times seeing God the Father, at times all three

Persons of the Trinity, and at times Our Lady, she who interceded for him and confirmed some of his discernments. In particular, he spoke to me about decisions over which he had spent forty days, saying Mass each day, and each day with many tears.[5] The question was whether a church could have any fixed income, and whether the Society could make use of that.

[101] The method that he followed while he was drafting the Constitutions was to say Mass each day, and to present to God the point that he was treating, and to pray over it. He always had tears at prayer and at Mass.

I wished to see all those papers on the *Constitutions*, and asked him to let me have them a while. He refused.

Appendix 1
Timeline of St. Ignatius's Life

1491   · Probably the year of Ignatius's birth.

1506?   · Ignatius goes to Arévalo as a page in the house of Juan
            Velázquez de Cuéllar (*c*.1460–1517).

1507   · Ignatius's father Beltrán de Loyola dies, and his brother
            Martín becomes lord of Castle Loyola. His mother had
            died sometime earlier.

1515   · He commits a crime that the civil prosecutor of Azpeitia
            calls "outrageous."

1517   · Velázquez dies. Ignatius enters the service of Antonio
            Manrique de Lara (d.1535), duke of Nájera and viceroy
            of Navarre.

1518   · Ignatius probably accompanies the duke to Valladolid
            for the recognition of Charles I as king of Castile and
            León (1500–58, r.1516–58).

1521   · Ignatius hastens with his brother Martín to defend
            Pamplona.
            · He is wounded, and the fortress surrenders.
            · Ignatius is carried to Castle Loyola. His conversion begins.
            · He has a vision of the Virgin Mary and Child.

1522   · Ignatius leaves home for Jerusalem, passing through
            Aránzazu and Navarrete.
            · He makes a private vow of chastity.
            · In Montserrat, he makes a general confession and vigil
            of arms before the Black Madonna.

1522 **(cont.)**	• He descends the mountain to Manresa, begins a life of prayer and penance. • He meets Inés Pascual and her son Juan. • The illumination at the River Cardoner.
1523	• He arrives in Barcelona, en route to Jerusalem. Meets Isabella Roser. • He arrives in Jerusalem. Remains a few weeks, then leaves for Spain.
1524	• He passes through Venice, returns to Barcelona. Briefly visits Manresa.
1525	• He studies Latin in Barcelona, engages in spiritual conversations and works of charity. • He recruits four companions, and refuses others like Juan Pascual and Miguel Torres (d.1593).
1526	• Ignatius goes to Alcalá to study the arts. Inquisitors are suspicious of him and his companions.
1527	• He and his companions are investigated several times. • He leaves Alcalá for Salamanca. Converses with the Dominicans at San Esteban. • Inquisitors' sentence: do not teach the distinction between venial and mortal sin. • He leaves Salamanca for Paris, via Barcelona. His four companions abandon him.
1528	• He arrives in Paris. Lodges in a hospice and studies Latin in the college of Montaigu. • He lacks funds, moves to the hospice of Saint-Jacques.
1529	• His first visit to Flanders. Meets Juan Luís Vives (1493–1540) in Bruges. • He gives the Exercises to Pedro de Peralta, Juan de Castro, and Amador de Elduayén.

1529	• He visits Rouen. Is threatened with a flogging. Transfers
(cont.)	to college of Saint-Barbe.
	• He begins to study philosophy. Meets Faber and Xavier.
1530	• He continues to study philosophy.
	• His second visit to Flanders.
1531	• He continues study philosophy.
	• His third visit to Flanders. Goes to London.
1532	• He receives the degree of bachelor of arts.
	• He meets Simão Rodrigues (*c.*1510–79).
1533	• He passes exams for licentiate in arts, is ranked thirty in a class of one hundred.
	• He begins to study theology.
	• He meets Diego Laínez and Alfonso Salmerón (1515–85).
1534	• He gives the Spiritual Exercises to Faber.
	• He gives the Spiritual Exercises to Laínez, Salmerón, Rodrigues, and Nicolás Bobadilla (*c.*1509–90).
	• He and six Companions make their vows at Montmartre.
	• He gives the Spiritual Exercises to Xavier.
1535	• He tries unsuccessfully to recruit Nadal.
	• He receives the diploma of master of arts.
	• He visits the inquisitor Valentin Liévin to defend himself against charge of heresy.
	• He leaves Paris for Azpeitia.
	• In Azpeitia, he preaches, teaches catechism, reconciles enemies, gives Exercises, helps the poor.
	• He visits families of the Companions in Obanos, Almazán, Sigüenza, Madrid, Toledo, and Valencia.

1536 • He reaches Venice, where he studies theology and gives the Exercises.
          • The other Companions leave Paris to join him in Venice.

1537 • The Companions minus Ignatius go to Rome to get papal permission for voyage to Jerusalem.
          • They agree to wait twelve months to find passage, from May 1537 to May 1538.
          • Ignatius, Xavier, Laínez, Rodrigues, Bobadilla, and Jean Codure (1508–41) are ordained priests.
          • Ignatius leaves for Rome with Faber and Laínez. His mystical experience at La Storta.

1538 • In Rome, Ignatius gives the Exercises, preaches, helps the poor.
          • When the twelve months end with no ship available, the other Companions come to Rome.
          • Miguel Landívar provokes another investigation of the Companions.
          • The Companions are exonerated and offer themselves to Paul III (1468–1549, r.1534–49).
          • They move to the house of Antonio Frangipani and remain there for a year and a half.
          • Ignatius says his first Mass in the basilica of St. Mary Major.
          • The Companions help hundreds of poor during a severe Roman winter.

1539 • The companions and other men deliberate becoming a formal religious order.
          • They write a proposed charter called the Formula of the Institute.
          • The pope sends some of them on missions in Italy.
          • Cardinal Gasparo Contarini (1483–1542) reads the Formula to Paul III, who orally approves it.

1540   • Xavier departs for Portugal and India.
             • Paul III approves the Society in the bull *Regimini militantis ecclesiae*.

1541   • Companions move to a house near the church of Our Lady of the Way.
             • Ignatius and Codure begin writing the *Constitutions*.
             • Ignatius is unanimously elected the first superior general of the Society of Jesus.
             • Companions make solemn vows in the papal basilica of Saint Paul-Outside-the-Walls.
             • Paul III gives the church of Our Lady of the Way to the Society.

1542   • Ignatius mediates dispute between Paul III and King John III of Portugal (1502–57, r.1521–57).
             • He sends Jesuits to establish a college at Coimbra and Padua.

1543   • Construction begins of Society's first house for professed, adjacent to Our Lady of the Way.

1544   • Ignatius works on the *Constitutions* and writes the extant portions of the *Spiritual Diary*.

1545   • Ignatius continues to have visions and other mystical experiences.
             • He receives Nadal into the Society.
             • Paul III requires Ignatius to receive vows of Roser and two other women.

1546   • Paul III in *Exponi nobis* permits the Society to accept
             Jesuit brothers.
           • Faber dies in Rome on his way to the Council of Trent
             (1545–63).
           • Roser and her two companions are dispensed from their
             vows.
           • Ignatius receives Francis Borgia (1510–72) into the
             Society.
           • The province of Portugal becomes the first in the
             Society.

1547   • Fr. Juan Polanco (1517–76) becomes Ignatius's
             secretary. Assists with composition of *Constitutions*.
           • Ignatius makes a spiritual pact between the Society and
             the Carthusians.
           • Fr. Antonio Araoz (1515–73) named the first provincial
             of Spain.
           • The college at Gandía becomes the first Jesuit university.

1548   • Ignatius continues working on the *Constitutions*.
           • On July 31, Paul III approves the *Spiritual Exercises*.

1549   • Ignatius sends first Jesuit missionaries to Brazil.
           • He deliberates founding the Roman College and a new
             Jesuit church.
           • He appoints Xavier the first provincial of the province
             of India.

1550   • Julius III (1487–1555, r.1550–55) in *Exposcit debitum*
             approves a revised Formula of the Institute.
           • First full draft of the *Constitutions* is given to the
             professed fathers in Rome for their critique.

1551   • Ignatius submits his resignation to the assembled
            fathers. All refuse except Fr. Andrés de Oviedo
            (1518–77).
         • The Roman College opens and quickly flourishes.
         • Ignatius sends a circular letter on how to establish Jesuit
            colleges.
         • Rodrigues's poor leadership of the province of Portugal
            causes a crisis.

1552   • Ignatius finishes the second full draft of the
            Constitutions.
         • He makes efforts to prevent Borgia from being named a
            cardinal.

1553   • Writes famous letter on obedience to the Jesuits of
            Coimbra.
         • Fr. Luís Gonçalves da Câmara arrives in Rome.
         • Ignatius begins to dictate his *Testament*.

1554   • Ignatius promotes a new mission to Ethiopia.
         • He divides Spain into three provinces: Castile, Aragon,
            Andalusia.
         • He continues editing the *Constitutions*.
         • He secretly admits Princess Juana (1479–1555),
            daughter of Charles V, into the Society.
         • He confirms Nadal as vicar general of the Society.

1555   • Gonçalves begins taking notes for his *Memoriale*. Jesuits
            in Rome number about 150.
         • Ignatius twice resumes dictation of the *Testament*.
         • Gian Pietro Carafa becomes Pope Paul IV (1476–1559,
            r.1555–59). Ignatius has fears.
         • Ignatius appoints Frs. Cristóbal de Madrid, Laínez, and
            Polanco as general assistants.

1556   • Ignatius is frequently sick. Entrusts governance of the
Society to Frs. Polanco and Madrid.
• On July 30, he has an intimation that he will soon die.
He asks Polanco to get a blessing from the pope.
• On July 31, shortly before 7:00 a.m., Ignatius dies
in the presence of Frs. Madrid and André des Freux
(1515–56).
• An autopsy is done the same day, and a death mask is
made.
• On August 1, after Vespers, Ignatius is buried in a side-
chapel of Our Lady of the Way.

1595   • Procedures begin for Ignatius's beatification.

1609   • Pope Paul V (1550–1621, r.1605–21) beatifies Ignatius.

1622   • Pope Gregory XV (1554–1623, r.1621–23) canonizes
Ignatius along with St. Francis Xavier, St. Teresa of Ávila
(1515–82), St. Philip Neri (1515–95), and St. Isidore the
Farmer (*c.*1070–1130).

Appendix 2
Classic Sources for Understanding
A Pilgrim's Testament

1. St. Luke's *Acts of the Apostles*

When Ignatius was alive, European Christians were taking renewed interest in the stories of St. Paul and the early church, especially as found in the *Acts of the Apostles*. One reason was that St. Luke describes Paul and the other disciples as traveling the known world to teach the Gospel. This was an attractive image in the sixteenth century, because European explorers had only recently discovered the New World and the Pacific Ocean. (In the same year Ignatius fell at Pamplona, the Portuguese explorer Ferdinand Magellan [1480–1521] died while trying to be the first to circle the globe.) Europeans were keenly aware of new lands waiting to hear the Gospel.

Another reason for the popularity of *Acts* was that St. Luke painted a romantic image of the early Christian Church (e.g., Acts 2:42–47). In Ignatius's day, many Catholics were disillusioned with the complacency and corruption that they saw—or at least thought that they saw—in the church. *Acts* gave them reason to hope that the church could return to her glory days. In fact, mystics at this time often prophesied that a saint was going to reform the church by gathering a group of twelve companions, just as Jesus had done.

For these reasons, readers will find in *A Pilgrim's Testament* allusions to the idea of Ignatius traveling the world like St. Paul and encountering the same kinds of challenges as Paul.

All biblical citations are the New American translation. On biblical themes in *A Pilgrim's Testament*, see John M. McManamon, *The Texts and Contexts of Ignatius Loyola's* Autobiography (New York: Fordham University Press, 2013). See also Thomas D. Stegman, "'Run That You May Obtain the Prize': Using St. Paul as a Resource for the Spiritual Exercises," *Studies in the Spirituality of Jesuits* 44, no. 4 (Winter 2012).

2. The Desert Fathers and Mothers

Starting in the late 200s, thousands of Christian men and women left
their homes in southern Europe and North Africa to become hermits
in the deserts of Egypt and Palestine. The first generation of hermits
sought complete solitude in caves or huts near a water source. In time,
however, hermits with reputations for wisdom and sanctity became
spiritual guides (*abbas* and *ammas*) for newcomers to the monastic vocation. The words and deeds of these spiritual masters (called
apophthegmata) were passed down from one generation of monks to
the next by way of an oral tradition, until anonymous Christians preserved them in writing sometime in the 500s. Two ancient collections
of *apophthegmata* had a tremendous impact on medieval spirituality, up to and including the spirituality of St. Ignatius. Today, these
collections remain a treasure trove of wisdom about discernment of
spirits and the early practice of spiritual direction.

> Sr. Benedicta Ward translated the two collections of sayings,
> giving them similar titles: *The Desert Fathers: Sayings of the
> Early Christian Monks* (London: Penguin, 2003), and *The Say-
> ings of the Desert Fathers: The Alphabetical Collection* (Kalam-
> azoo, MI: Cistercian Publications, 1975). In this book, citations
> begin with *Ward*, then the abbreviated title of the book, then
> page number. See Heinrich Bacht, "Early Monastic Elements
> in Ignatian Spirituality: Toward Clarifying Some Fundamental
> Concepts of the Exercises," in *Ignatius of Loyola: His Personality
> and Spiritual Heritage 1556–1956*, ed. Friedrich Wulf, 200–36
> (St. Louis, MO: Institute of Jesuit Sources, 1977); and Hugo
> Rahner, "Ignatius and the Ascetic Tradition of the Fathers," in
> *Ignatius the Theologian*, trans. Michael Barry, 32–52 (New York:
> Herder and Herder, 1968).

3. St. Athanasius of Alexandria's (*c.*296–373) *The Life of St. Antony*

Athanasius wrote his book the year after Antony's death, with the intention of popularizing the desert movement among Christians in the Roman Empire. He succeeded spectacularly. The book became the first Christian bestseller, inspiring countless thousands of Christians to go to the desert, either to seek advice from these spiritual masters, or to become hermits themselves. That is why the church traditionally credits St. Antony (*c.*251–356), somewhat incorrectly, as the first Christian monk.

Athanasius's book had a tremendous impact on medieval hagiographies, including *A Pilgrim's Testament*. In the *Life*, for example, Antony speaks to fellow monks about discernment of spirits, and he gives them a description of consolations and desolations that bears a striking resemblance to what Ignatius will write in the *Spiritual Exercises* some 1,200 years later.

> Two English translations of the *Life of St. Antony* are: Robert T. Meyer, *Saint Athanasius:* The Life of St. Antony, Ancient Christian Writers Series 10 (New York: Newman Press, 1950); and Robert C. Gregg, *Athanasius:* The Life of Antony *and the* Letter to Marcellinus, Classics of Western Spirituality Series (New York: Paulist Press, 1980). Traditionally, the *Life* is divided into the same numbered sections, and these are used by both translations. In this book, citations of the *Life* use those numbers after a section symbol (§).

4. John Cassian's (*c.*360–*c.*435) *The Conferences* and *The Institutes*

Stories of the *abbas* and *ammas* fascinated Cassian since his youth. When he was in his twenties, he left home in modern-day Romania to visit and interview famous monks in Bethlehem and Egypt. *The Conferences* is a collection of those interviews; each chapter includes a conversation with an *abba* on a subject like prayer, asceticism, or discernment of spirits. Later, Cassian wrote *The Institutes* as a guide for monks in modern-day France who wished to follow Egyptian spirituality and practice. In *The Institutes*, one finds Cassian's famous treatment of the *eight deadly thoughts*, which later writers reduced to the *seven deadly sins* that Christians know today. Cassian's work exerted a profound impact on Christian spiritualities, up to and including that of St. Ignatius.

> For translations, see Boniface Ramsey, *John Cassian:* The Conferences, Ancient Christian Writers Series 57 (New York: Newman Press, 1997), and *John Cassian:* The Institutes, Ancient Christian Writers Series 58 (New York: Newman Press, 2000). Citations of these works refer to their chapters and sections as found in the Ramsey translations. See also Lawrence S. Cunningham, "Cassian's Hero and Discernment: Some Reflections," in *Finding God in All Things: Essays in Honor of Michael J. Buckley, S.J.*, ed. Michael J. Himes and Stephen J. Pope, 231–43 (New York: Crossroads, 1996).

5. Ludolph of Saxony's (*c.*1295–1378) *The Life of Jesus Christ*

Ignatius read this book during his recuperation at Castle Loyola. Ludolph recounts Jesus's life in a way that synthesizes the four Gospels. He incorporates the teachings of saints and theologians throughout the centuries in order to elaborate upon Jesus's stories and sayings.

> Ludolph divided his *Life* into two parts. For an English translation in four volumes, see Milton T. Walsh, *Ludolph of Saxony: The* Life of Jesus Christ, *Part One*, vol. 1, chapters 1–40 (Collegeville, MN: Liturgical Press, 2018), and *The* Life of Jesus Christ, *Part One*, vol. 2, chapters 41–92 (Collegeville, MN: Liturgical Press, 2019), and *The* Life of Jesus Christ, *Part Two*, vol. 3, chapters 1–57 (Collegeville, MN: Liturgical Press, 2020). *The* Life of Jesus

Christ, *Part Two*, vol. 4, chapters 58–89, is scheduled to be published in 2021. In this book, citations of the *Life* refer to volume and page number of Milton's translation. See also Paul Shore, "The *Vita Christi* of Ludolph of Saxony and Its Influence on the *Spiritual Exercises* of Ignatius of Loyola," *Studies in the Spirituality of Jesuits* 30, no. 1 (January 1998), and Milton T. Walsh, "To Be Always Thinking Somehow about Jesus: The Prologue of Ludolph's *Vita Christi*," *Studies in the Spirituality of Jesuits* 43, no. 1 (Spring 2011).

6. Jacobus de Voragine's (*c.*1230–*c.*1298) *The Golden Legend*

This was the second book that Ignatius read during his recovery. The original title that Jacobus had given it was *Legenda sanctorum*, or "Readings of the Saints." He compiled short lives of many saints, using medieval sources that were a mixture of fact and legend. His book was immensely popular and greatly influenced Catholic iconography.

Specifically, Ignatius read an edition of the *Golden Legend* that the Cistercian Gauberto María Vagad had translated into colloquial Spanish in the late fifteenth century; Vagad added his own prologue. Its title was *Flos sanctorum*, or "Flower of the Saints" (*FontNarr.* 2:187).

William Granger Ryan (1905–96) translated the *Golden Legend* into English. See *Jacobus de Voragine:* The Golden Legend; *Readings on the Saints*, 2 vols. (Princeton: Princeton University Press, 1993). Citations refer to volume and page number of Ryan's translation.

7. Thomas à Kempis's (1380–1471) *The Imitation of Christ*

The *Imitation* is perhaps the most popular devotional work in Christian history. The author desired to help readers cultivate a personal, heartfelt relationship with Jesus, and so he depicts Jesus speaking directly to readers with tender words of encouragement and counsel.

During Ignatius's brief stay at Montserrat (*Test.* §17–18), the confessor for the pilgrims, Fr. Jean Cannon introduced Ignatius to this book, which remained a favorite throughout Ignatius's life. As superior general, Ignatius read a chapter from it every day, and he often recommended it to others (Eaglestone §97–98). In particular, its themes of self-conquest, personal intimacy with Jesus, and *pure intention*—which means a Christian doing something solely for love of God and for his glory, without any degree of self-interest—appear prominently in the *Spiritual Exercises* and the *Constitutions* of the Jesuit order.

> There are many English translations of the *Imitation*. Recommended is Harold C. Gardiner, ed., *The Imitation of Christ* (New York: Image Books, 1983). Traditionally, the *Imitation* is divided into four books, each with numbered chapters; citations in this book refer to these. See also Maximilian von Habsburg, *Catholic and Protestant Translations of the* Imitatio Christi, *1425–1650: From Late Medieval Classic to Early Modern Bestseller* (London: Routledge, 2016); two chapters pertain to the influence of the *Imitatio* on Ignatius and the early Jesuits.

8. Jean Gerson's (1363–1429) *Snares of the Devil*

Gerson was a famous writer on the discernment of spirits, and he came to the defense of St. Joan of Arc (*c.*1412–31) against those who did not believe that her mystical experiences were genuine. *Snares* is an amusing list of ways that Christians can rationalize and deceive themselves in the spiritual life. There is no evidence that Ignatius read it, although given his interest in discernment and his respect for Gerson—whom he mistakenly believed was the author of the *Imitation of Christ*—he likely did. Either way, *Snares* shares many similarities to the *Testament* and *Spiritual Exercises*. It is included here as a good example of the general tradition that shaped Ignatius.

> An unknown translator under the pseudonym "Beta" provided what appears to be the only readily available edition of *Snares*

of the Devil in English (London: Thomas Richardson and Son, 1883). The translation is no longer under copyright, and therefore can be downloaded for free from the internet at www.internetarchive.org. The text contains five chapters, each with numbered sections. Citations of *Snares* refer to these.

9. *The Spiritual Exercises*

Ignatius dictated *A Pilgrim's Testament* for the purpose of teaching and edifying future Jesuits. It makes sense, therefore, that he used the *Testament* to illustrate the wisdom found in the *Spiritual Exercises*.

There are many editions of the *Spiritual Exercises*, but most of them number its individual sections in the same manner. A translation with excellent notes is *The Spiritual Exercises of Saint Ignatius*, ed. and trans. George E. Ganss (St. Louis, MO: Institute of Jesuit Sources, 1992). See also Javier Melloni, *The Exercises of St. Ignatius Loyola in the Western Tradition*, trans. Michael Ivens (Leominster: Gracewing, 2000).

10. The Letters of St. Ignatius

Today, over seven thousand letters written by Ignatius, or by Jesuit secretaries on his behalf, are preserved in archives throughout the world. Ignatius wrote them to friends and fellow Jesuits, as well as to popes, kings, bishops, noblewomen, and governors. The letters are invaluable for shedding light on what Ignatius meant in various passages in *A Pilgrim's Testament* and the *Spiritual Exercises*.

For a translation of several hundred of the most significant letters, see *Ignatius of Loyola: Letters and Instructions*, ed. Martin E. Palmer, John W. Padberg, and John L. McCarthy (St. Louis, MO: Institute of Jesuit Sources, 2006). All citations of the letters begin with the number of the letter as found in the Monumenta Historica Societatis Iesu, followed by the page number of its translation (if available) in the Palmer edition.

11. The Earlier Lives of Ignatius Written by Diego Laínez and Juan Polanco

Polanco was a Jesuit who worked as Ignatius's secretary. In 1547, he asked one of the priests who had helped found the Society, Laínez, to write down what he knew about Ignatius's story. Polanco believed it was important to record all that he could about Ignatius, so that future Jesuits could model their own lives and ministries on their saintly founder.

Laínez was a brilliant theologian. When he received Polanco's letter, he was extremely busy at the Council of Trent, serving as a consultant for bishops who were discussing matters concerning the Protestant Reformation. Nevertheless, Laínez managed to send Polanco a long letter in which he recounted what he remembered of Ignatius's life. For the most part, it would have been based on what Ignatius himself had told Laínez over the years.

It seems that Polanco was dissatisfied with Laínez's letter, because shortly after he received it, he began writing his own life of Ignatius, using Laínez's letter as the foundation. Polanco generally absorbed Laínez's text verbatim, but he did change some details, expand some stories, and add new stories.

Gonçalves probably consulted these lives while he was preparing to dictate to scribes his final version of *A Pilgrim's Testament*. There are strong similarities between the three texts, which makes the differences between them all the more significant.

See Joseph A. Munitiz, *The First Biographies of St. Ignatius Loyola: Diego Laínez and Juan Polanco* (Campion Hall, Oxford: Way Books, 2019). Citations begin with "Munitiz," followed by *First Biographies*, and page numbers.

12. Pedro de Ribadeneira's (1527–1611) *The Life of Ignatius of Loyola*

Ten years after Ignatius died, the second superior general of the Society of Jesus, Laínez, asked Fr. Ribadeneira to write another life of Ignatius. Laínez was dissatisfied with *A Pilgrim's Testament*, probably because of all the important events that Ignatius and Gonçalves failed to mention. He wanted a book that was more polished and that covered the entirety of Ignatius's life, so that it could serve as the "official" life of Ignatius for future Jesuits. Ribadeneira wrote the first edition between 1567 and 1569, using *A Pilgrim's Testament* as a source. He revised and expanded it twice more after that, in 1583 and 1586.

> See Claude Pavur, ed., *Pedro de Ribadeneira, S.J.: The Life of Ignatius of Loyola* (St. Louis, MO: Institute of Jesuit Sources, 2014). Citations of the *Life* begin with "Pavur," followed by page number.

13. The Writings of St. Peter Faber

Faber was a pious farm boy from France who met Ignatius at the University of Paris, and who became his first recruit for the future Society of Jesus. Faber grew into a deeply holy man with a winning personality, and he endeared himself to almost everyone who knew him. In fact, Ignatius once remarked that, of all the early Jesuits, Faber knew best how to direct people in the *Spiritual Exercises*. Faber's spiritual diary reveals the private thoughts and feelings of a man who loved God and the Society of Jesus. It also reveals how he understood Ignatius's spirituality and values.

> See Edmond C. Murphy and Martin E. Palmer, eds., *The Spiritual Writings of Pierre Favre: The* Memoriale *and Selected Letters and Instructions* (St. Louis, MO: Institute of Jesuit Sources, 1996). Citations of this text begin with "Murphy," followed by page numbers.

14. The *Memoriale* of Luís Gonçalves da Câmara

When Ignatius was superior general, Gonçalves followed him around the Jesuit headquarters for nine months, observing all that he said and did. Gonçalves then recorded it for posterity. He wanted future Jesuits to have as clear an idea as possible of the man that Ignatius was.

> See Alexander Eaglestone and Joseph A. Munitiz, eds., *Remembering Iñigo: Glimpses of the Life of Saint Ignatius of Loyola; The* Memoriale *of Luís Gonçalves da Câmara* (Leominster: Gracewing, 2004). Each of Gonçalves's entries is numbered. Citations of the *Memoriale* begin with "Eaglestone," followed by a section symbol (§) and one of those numbers.

15. The Writings of St. Teresa of Ávila

Teresa is generally considered the greatest female writer of the sixteenth century, and she holds the distinction of being one of four female doctors of the church, meaning writers who have had a profound impact on how Catholic Christians understand their faith. She began to write her autobiography in 1565, nine years after Ignatius's death. Teresa never met Ignatius, but several early Jesuits were her confessors and spiritual directors, and she developed an admiration for the Society of Jesus. In *A Pilgrim's Testament*, her writings will be cited in order to illustrate how certain ideas of Ignatius were part of a broader Catholic religious culture at this time.

> See Kieran Kavanaugh and Otilio Rodriguez, eds., *The Collected Works of St. Teresa of Ávila*, 3 vols., 2nd ed. (Washington, DC: Institute of Carmelite Studies Publications, 1976–85). *The Book of Her Life* is found in 1:53–365. Citations refer to volume and page numbers.

Appendix 3
About Citations of the MHSI

Almost all the writings of St. Ignatius and other early, prominent Jesuits have been critically edited in their original languages, in a multi-volume series called Monumenta Historica Societatis Iesu. In an effort to make this edition of *A Pilgrim's Testament* as friendly as possible for students and non-specialists, I refrain from citing the MHSI whenever English translations are available. Otherwise, these abbreviations refer readers to volumes of the MHSI:

Bobadilla	*Nicolai Alphonsi de Bobadilla sacerdotis e Societate Jesu gesta et scripta.* Madrid, 1913 (no. 46 of the series).
Broët	*Epistolae PP. Paschasii Broëti, Claudii Jaji, Joannis Codurii et Simonis Rodericii.* Madrid, 1903. (no. 24)
Chronicon	Juan Alfonso de Polanco, *Vita Ignatii Loiolae et rerum Societatis Iesu historica* (the *Chronicon*), 6 vols. Madrid, 1894–98 (nos. 1, 3, 5, 7, 9, 11).
Const.	*Monumenta ignatiana: Sancti Ignatii de Loyola; Constitutiones Societatis Jesu.* 3 vols. Rome, 1934–38.
Epist.	*Monumenta ignatiana: Sancti Ignatii de Loyola Societatis Jesu fundatoris epistolae et instructiones*, 12 vols. Madrid, 1903–11 (nos. 22, 26, 28, 29, 31, 33, 34, 36, 37, 39, 40, 42).
EpistMixtae	*Epistolae mixtae ex variis Europae loci ab anno 1537 ad 1556 scriptae*, 5 vols. Madrid, 1898–1901 (nos. 12, 14, 17, 18, 20).
Faber	*B. Petri Fabri primi sacerdotis e Societate Jesu epistolae, memoriale et processus.* Madrid, 1914 (no. 48).

FontDoc.	*Monumenta Ignatiana: Fontes documentales de S. Ignatio de Loyola.* Rome, 1977 (no. 115).
FontNarr.	*Fontes narrativi de S. Ignatio de Loyola et de Societatis Jesus initiis,* 4 vols. Rome, 1943–65 (nos. 66, 73, 85, 93).
Laínez	*Epistolae et acta Patris Jacobi Lainii,* 8 vols. Madrid, 1912–17 (nos. 44, 45, 47, 49, 50, 51, 53, 55).
Nadal	*Epistolae P. Hieronymi Nadal Societatis Jesu ab anno 1546 ad 1577,* 5 vols. Madrid, 1898–1905. Comentarii de Instituto Societatis Jesu. Rome, 1962 (nos. 13, 15, 21, 27, 90).
Polanco	*Polanci complementa: Epistolae et commentaria P. Joannis Alphonsi de Polanco,* 2 vols. Madrid, 1916–17.
Scripta	*Monumenta ignatiana: Scripta de Sancto Ignacio de Loyola,* 2 vols. Madrid, 1904–18 (nos. 25, 56).

The original Spanish and Italian copy of *A Pilgrim's Testament*, together with the Latin translation of Fr. Hannibal du Coudret, is critically edited in *FontNarr.* 1:323–507.

In the MHSI, scholars gave numbers to individual sections of Ignatius's most important works, such as the *Spiritual Exercises,* the *Constitutions* of the Jesuit order, and *A Pilgrim's Testament.* Most modern translations of these works include those numbers, to help readers find specific passages more easily.

In *A Pilgrim's Testament,* those numbers appear in square brackets at the beginning of each section. In the introduction and endnotes of this book, whenever readers see the abbreviation *Test.* followed by a section symbol (§), it refers to those bracketed numbers.

Similarly, the abbreviations *SpirEx.* and *Cons.,* followed by section symbols, will refer readers to specific passages in the *Spiritual Exercises* and Jesuit *Constitutions.* Again, these numbers will be accurate regardless of the translation of the *Exercises* or *Constitutions* that one is using.

Notes

Foreword of Fr. Jerónimo Nadal

1. Fr. Nadal refers to the desert fathers and mothers, saintly hermits living in the deserts of Egypt and Palestine in the fourth to sixth centuries. For various reasons, they gradually began living in closer proximity to each other, until the point that they lived together in communities with their own rules and spiritualities. It was the beginning of Christian monasteries, and by extension, of Catholic religious orders. In the 1500s, Catholics were fascinated by the stories of the desert fathers and mothers, and their influence is evident in the writings of Ignatius and other early Jesuits. In that light, Nadal's comment provides an important key for interpreting the spirituality found in *A Pilgrim's Testament*. See appendix 2, 2–4.

2. In *The Golden Legend*, St. Dominic "called together the twelve friars of the priory at Bologna, and, so as not to leave them orphaned and without a heritage, gave them his testament [*testamentum*]" (Ryan 2:113).

3. Nadal erred about the year; it was 1552. "Now I was higher than heaven" alludes to St. Paul's description of his own mystical ecstasies (2 Cor. 12:1–5). Paul had mixed feelings. He wanted to tell the Gentiles about his mystical experiences in order to edify them and establish his authority as one really sent by God. At the same time, he did not want to appear conceited. Ignatius faced the same dilemma, which is why he was cagey with Nadal, and why he procrastinated about dictating his memoirs. Yet like Paul, he finally decided that the edification of others took priority. To remain silent would not have been real humility, but rather false humility. See *SpirEx.* §351 and Ignatius's letter 7 to Sr. Teresa Rejadell (trans. Palmer 19–20). See also the description of monks interrupting St. Antony from a mystical experience in *Life of St. Antony* §82.

4. Fr. Juan Alfonso de Polanco was Ignatius's secretary in Rome. Fr. Ponce Cogordan (1500–82) was the house procurator. Polanco's organizational skills and penchant for preserving documents are two reasons why modern historians enjoy such a wealth of sources on the early Society of Jesus.

5.   Nadal implies that it was his demonstration of indifference that swayed
      Ignatius: instead of insisting on his own opinion that Ignatius dictate
      his memoirs, he expressed a freedom to desire and choose whatever
      was for God's greater glory. Ignatius would have been pleased with this,
      because he had counseled Christians to practice this indifference in
      the *Spiritual Exercises* (§23). However, Gonçalves affirms in his own
      foreword that Ignatius agreed to dictate his memoirs only after Ignatius
      had seen how sharing his struggles with vanity had helped to alleviate
      Gonçalves's distress about his own struggles with vanity. There is no
      reason why both incidents could not have influenced Ignatius. The
      important point is that the greater good of souls was the decisive factor
      in each.

6.   Nadal called Ignatius's memoirs *Acta Patris Ignatii* (Acts of Our Father
      Ignatius). The word *Acts* would have reminded readers of St. Luke's
      Acts of the Apostles. In the ancient church, the word also referred to the
      collected stories of early Christian martyrs, the *Acta martyrum*. In later
      centuries, *Acts* often referred to the collected stories of all saints, not
      just martyrs. The Jesuit scholar Fr. Heribert Rosweyde (1569–1629), for
      example, compiled a multi-volume work entitled *Acta sanctorum* (Acts
      of the Saints). Nadal's title "Acts of Our Father Ignatius" implied that
      the purpose of the text was to edify and instruct Jesuits, as opposed to
      simply satisfying their curiosity about their founder's life.

7.   Gonçalves and Fr. Amador Rebelo (1538–1622) tutored Sebastian of
      Portugal (1554–78, r.1557–78), who became king at the age of three.
      Rebelo was a nephew of Simão Rodrigues, one of the founding fathers
      of the Society. Rebelo often cared for Gonçalves, whose health was del-
      icate, and he was a favorite in the royal court.

8.   Fr. Hannibal du Coudret (1525–99) was born in Savoy. His *De primis
      latinae grammatices rudimentis libellus* was one of the first scholarly
      works written by Jesuits. He helped to establish the college in Messina
      in 1548, and while professor of Greek at the Roman College (1558–61),
      he translated *A Pilgrim's Testament* into Latin.

Foreword of Fr. Luís Gonçalves da Câmara

1.   Today, people often understand *vainglory* (or simply *vanity*) and *pride* as synonymous. In the Catholic tradition, however, they are distinct. Vanity means that people are insecure about their abilities and worth, and thus crave attention and adulation from others. Pride means that people have inflated confidence in their abilities and worth, and thus disdain attention and help from others. Cassian gives a separate chapter to each in *The Institutes* (chapters 11 and 12; trans. Ramsey 239–79). Vanity was Ignatius's lifelong temptation. He knew that if he told people about his pilgrimage, they would praise him as a holy man, and he did not want to fall into the trap of telling people about the pilgrimage precisely for their praise (see *Test.* §36).

2.   On the significance of tears in *A Pilgrim's Testament*, see Epilogue of Fr. Gonçalves, n. 5

3.   The word "duty" (*deber*) is significant. Once Ignatius realizes that sharing his story will serve the greater glory of God, it becomes something that he is obliged to do in conscience. It is no longer a question of his personal preference. Thus Ignatius writes in the *Spiritual Exercises*, "we ought [*deber*] to desire and choose only that which is more conducive to the end for which we are created" (§23).

4.   In the Middle Ages, writers frequently warned Christians not to be presumptuous about how long they would live. See *Life of St. Antony* §16, 19; *Life of Jesus Christ* (trans. Walsh 1:395–99), *Imitation of Christ* 1:23, 25.

5.   *A Pilgrim's Testament* does not contain a detailed chapter about the sins of Ignatius's youth. Apparently, Ignatius and/or Gonçalves had second thoughts about including it, for fear of scandalizing readers. Circumstantial evidence suggests it was Gonçalves, because he noted elsewhere that Ignatius had often recounted his past sins to Jesuits when he believed that it would console them (Eaglestone §78–79). Gonçalves also noted that he himself once hesitated to dictate a story to a Jesuit scribe for fear of scandalizing the scribe (Eaglestone §256b).

6.   Gonçalves used different scribes for each session, resulting in different handwriting. In the original manuscript of ninety-six leaves, the first scribe wrote chapters 1 and 2. A second scribe wrote chapter 3 in smaller handwriting. The first scribe then resumed until *Test.* §79. An Italian wrote the remainder of the text.

7. The Church Fathers taught that Christians' manner of speech and exterior comportment are reliable indicators of their spiritual maturity and even of their orthodoxy (see Thomas H. Clancy, *Conversational Word of God: A Commentary on the Doctrine of St. Ignatius of Loyola concerning Spiritual Conversation, with Four Early Jesuit Texts* [St. Louis, MO: Institute of Jesuit Sources, 1978], 16–18, 38–44). Thus, Ignatius wanted Jesuits to be known for sobriety in their speech: they should avoid jocularity, exaggeration, and rhetorical flair. Gonçalves frequently noted Ignatius's own example in that regard (Eaglestone §26–27, 192, 195, 202–4, 227, 250, 289, 291, 379, 401). The popular myth that Ignatius used to say "Go and set the world on fire!" is quite contrary to his real style of communication, and it has no reliable basis in the sources (see Barton T. Geger, "Myths, Misquotes, and Misconceptions about St. Ignatius Loyola," *Jesuit Higher Education* 5, no. 1 [2016]: 7–20, here 9–10).

8. Prester John was a legendary Christian king, the location of whose kingdom was supposedly lost to history. In the 1500s, Christians often identified him with the king of Abyssinia (modern Ethiopia). Nadal refers to the fact that Pope Julius III had asked Ignatius to send Jesuit missionaries to Ethiopia in order to bring its Monophysite Christians into full communion with the Catholic Church. Ignatius expressed great enthusiasm for this mission (letter 5205, trans. Palmer 530–31, 544–49).

9. Pope Marcellus II (1501–55, r.1555) was elected on April 9 and died on May 1. He had shown promise as a church reformer and friend of the Society, and Ignatius was saddened at his sudden death.

10. When Ignatius heard the news that Cardinal Gian Pietro Carafa (1476–1559) had been elected Pope Paul IV (r.1555–59), he paled and shuddered (Eaglestone §93). Years earlier, Ignatius had presumed to give Carafa unsolicited critiques of the Theatine order that Carafa had co-founded with St. Cajetan (1480–1547). Now, Ignatius feared that a resentful Paul IV might rescind papal permission for the Society of Jesus.

11. A small building affixed to the Roman College that Jesuits used as an infirmary for the poor who were suffering from a grain famine and the cold weather (*Chronicon* 1:65).

12. Gonçalves had poor eyesight, so he kept edging closer to Ignatius to see his facial expressions. But he was breaking one of the "Rules of

Modesty" (*Regulae modestiae*) that Ignatius had written for Jesuits, namely that they should not stare at faces of other people, especially of those in authority. An English translation of the rules is found in Clancy, *Conversational Word of God*, 70–71, and Eaglestone §22.

1. Pamplona and Loyola (May 1521 to Late February 1522)

1. "Vanities" (*vanidades*). Ignatius's opening line in the *Testament* alludes to the first sentence of his favorite book, the *Imitation of Christ*: "Of the Imitation or Following of Christ and the Despising of All Vanities of the World" (trans. Gardiner 3). *De imitatione Christi et contemptu mundi omniumque eius vanitatum.* Ignatius gives his age as twenty-six; in reality, he probably was closer to thirty.

2. The walls of the fortress had not been completed. The fortress no longer exists, but a plaque on the ground marks the location of Ignatius's fall.

3. In the Middle Ages, Catholics could confess to laypersons if death was imminent and priests were not available. The confession was not sacramental. It was meant to demonstrate true contrition.

4. The date of Ignatius's injury was probably May 20, 1521. The projectile was likely chain shot, meaning two metal balls connected by a chain that extended after exiting the cannon.

5. A litter was a large wooden box with a door and windows, and with a bed or seat inside. It was carried by four men, two in front and two in back, by means of long wooden poles on either side. The jostling of the litter as it was carried over the mountain roads would have been excruciating for Ignatius's broken leg.

6. When Ignatius refers to other butcheries that he endured patiently, he was not necessarily referring to other surgeries on his leg. As superior general, he suffered crippling stomach pains. An incompetent doctor tried to cure him by wrapping him in heavy blankets and closing the windows, all in the middle of a Roman summer. Ignatius nearly died of thirst, but Jesuits rescued him by calling for another doctor. All the while, according to Gonçalves, Ignatius uttered no complaint (Eaglestone §35). On another occasion, a thug beat Ignatius nearly to death; he had been hired by men who resented Ignatius's attempts to convert some unchaste nuns. During his two month recovery, according to Juan Pascual (see Ch. 4, n. 11), Ignatius made no complaint (*Scripta* 2:91). These and similar stories about "no complaints" suggest that, in *Test.*

§2, Ignatius is underscoring the importance of Christian patience in general (see Ch. 1, n 8).

7.   The feast days were June 24 and June 29, respectively.

8.   Ignatius does not recount this story to impress readers with his machismo. The word *patience* (*paciencia* in Spanish) denoted a pre-eminent Christian virtue. Since the ancient church, it meant enduring sufferings and setbacks, whether great or small, with tranquility and charity. The Church Fathers wrote treatises on patience, and they praised it as the mother of all Christian virtues. "So is patience set over the things of God," wrote Tertullian (*c*.155–*c*.240), "that one can obey no precept, fulfill no work well-pleasing to the Lord, if estranged from it" (*De patientia* §1), and again, "Patience is God's nature" (§3). Thus, Ignatius lists patience among the virtues that he lacked in *Test.* §14, even though it contradicted what he said earlier about "his normal patience" (§4). In the *Constitutions*, Ignatius wanted Jesuits to ask candidates for the Society: "Is he determined and ready to accept and suffer with patience [*patiencia*], through the help of God's grace, any such injuries, mockeries, and affronts entailed by the wearing of this uniform of Christ our Lord [...] while returning them not evil for evil, but evil for good?" (§102). On patience in the Christian tradition, see David Baily Harned, *Patience: How We Wait Upon the World* (Cambridge, MA: Cowley, 1997). Pope Francis made patience a prominent theme in *Evangelii Gaudium* (November 24, 2013).

9.   On the two books, see appendix 2, 5–6.

10.   Scholars debate the identity of this woman. A likely candidate is Princess Catalina (1485–1536), the charming younger sister of Emperor Charles V, who was then in her early teens. She later married King John III of Portugal, a generous patron of the Jesuits. But many years later, Ignatius admitted to having been infatuated with the beauty of his sister-in-law Magdalena de Araoz, who was the lady of Castle Loyola when Ignatius was recuperating there (*Scripta* 2:435–36; Hugo Rahner, ed., *St. Ignatius of Loyola: Letters to Women* [New York: Herder and Herder, 1960], 115–16). She owned the books that Ignatius read.

11.   Laínez and Polanco provide a different account of Ignatius's conversion, namely that he chose to read the books only after he had made a decision to follow Christ, and that he did this for the specific purpose of reinforcing what he already knew was a good decision (Munitiz,

First Biographies, 3, 42). These alternative accounts, in which solitude and reflection were enough to provoke a conversion in Ignatius, suggest that dissatisfaction with his old life, and perhaps even a religious vocation, had been rumbling in him long before Pamplona. This interpretation finds an intriguing parallel in *SpirEx.* §100, where Ignatius advises retreatants not to read the lives of Christ and the saints during the First Week (when they are reflecting on their personal history), but they should during the Second Week (after they have already made a decision to respond to the call of the King in *SpirEx.* §91–98).

12. Today, one often hears that "comparisons are odious," but medieval spiritualities greatly esteemed holy desires to imitate the saints. St. Athanasius wrote in the prologue to the *Life of St. Antony*: "You have entered on a fine contest with the monks of Egypt, intending as you do to measure up to or even to surpass them in your disciple of virtue. [...] One may justly praise this purpose of yours, and as you ask in prayer, may God bring your requests to fulfillment" (trans. Gregg 29). Ignatius exhorted young Jesuits to a similar competitive spirit in letter 169, trans. Palmer 166–70. See also *Imitation of Christ* 1:28.

13. St. Francis of Assisi (1182–1226) and St. Dominic Guzmán (1170–1221) founded two illustrious religious orders. In the *Golden Legend*, Dominic has a mystical vision in which Mary presents both him and Francis to Jesus; both saints recognize each other as kindred spirits in the service of reforming the church (trans. Ryan 2:47–48, 225).

    Scholars debate the moment when Ignatius first thought of founding a religious order, or more specifically, the Society with its distinguishing characteristics. In centuries past, Jesuits often claimed, without solid evidence, that Ignatius had seen the future Society in his mystical illumination at the Cardoner (*Test.* §30). Modern writers often over-correct by asserting that a religious order never entered Ignatius's mind until 1538, when his plans to return to Jerusalem came to naught (*Test.* §94). At a minimum, the evidence is clear that Ignatius was committed to forming an apostolic group as early as his studies in Barcelona. And of course, the stories of Francis and Dominic in the *Flos Sanctorum* could easily have sparked daydreams in Ignatius about founding an order while he was still recuperating.

14. According to Nadal, the Egyptian hermit St. Humphrey (or Onufrius) (*fl.* fourth or fifth century) made a particular impression on Ignatius.

See Pedro Leturia, "El influjo de San Onofre en San Ignacio a Base de un texto inédito de Nadal," *Manresa* 2 (1926): 224–38. Humphrey does not appear in the *Golden Legend*, but rather in the particular edition of the *Flos sanctorum* read by Ignatius. See appendix 2, 6, and Joseph Conwell, *Impelling Spirit: Revisiting a Founding Experience, 1539, Ignatius of Loyola and His Companions; An Exploration into the Spirit and Aims of the Society of Jesus as Revealed in the Founders' Proposed Papal Letter Approving the Society* (Chicago: Loyola Press, 1997), 525n15.

15. In *Test. §7*, Ignatius is "reasoning to himself" (*razonando consigo*), and in *Test. §8*, he notes consolations and desolations. In the *Spiritual Exercises*, discernment of God's will requires attention to both reason and affectivity. Scholars have long debated the proper roles and relative weight that Ignatius gave to each, especially in the context of the "Three Times for Making an Election" (*SpirEx.* §175–78). Notably in that regard, Laínez and Polanco remarked that Ignatius's idea of giving his life to Christ, "in addition to being good," also left him with subjective consolations (Munitiz, *First Biographies*, 2, 42). It was perhaps a subtle insinuation that reason alone would have been sufficient for Ignatius to make his decision.

16. Comment by Gonçalves in the margins: "This was his first reflection on the things of God. Later, when he composed the Exercises, this was his starting point in clarifying the matter of diversity of spirits" (*FontNarr.* 1:372).

17. "Consolation" (*consolación*). A quasi-technical term in Catholic theology of the sixteenth century. In general, it meant a warm, pleasant, affective experience within a person that God stimulates for the purpose of edifying the person or communicating his will; as opposed to the ordinary pleasant emotions that one experiences by virtue of being human. Consolations are distinguishable from ordinary emotions in terms of: (1) their intensity, which is disproportionate to whatever stimulated them; (2) the fact that they remain long after the stimuli are gone; (3) they make burdens and sufferings seem light, even welcome, in the service of God; and (4) they generate greater faith, hope, and love in the person. Ignatius's consolations exhibit all these qualities in the *Testament*. Ignatius provides his own description of consolations in *SpirEx.* §316.

Desolations, in contrast, are unpleasant affective states that lead one to "obtuseness of soul, turmoil within it, an impulsive motion toward low and earthly things, or disquiet from various agitations and temptations. These move one toward lack of faith and leave one without hope and without love. One is completely listless, tepid, and unhappy, and feels separated from our Creator and Lord" (*SpirEx*. §317, trans. Ganss, *Exercises*, 122). Ignatius's description of consolations and desolations bears a resemblance to St. Athanasius's description of the same (*Life of St. Antony* §36).

In the sixteenth century, many spiritual writers advocated that Christians pay little or no attention to consolations, on the grounds that they were too easily misinterpreted (e.g., *Test*. §19, 26) and led to overly subjective and privatized convictions about God's will. And like the feeling of falling in love, consolations have a heady, addictive quality that Christians can be tempted to seek for its own sake, as opposed to loving and serving God because reason and revelation are clear that God is worthy of that love and service (see Ch. 2, n 8). For that reason, some spiritual masters such as St. Claude la Colombiere (1641–82) prayed that God not give them consolations at all. Ignatius, however, gave consolations a prominent place in his spiritual doctrine: in the discernment of spirits, they are evidence that an idea or desire is from God (*SpirEx*. §318, 329); in discernment of God's will, they provide direction regarding what to desire and choose (*SpirEx*. §175–76), and they make Christians' fulfilment of their duties feel less compulsory, more joyful (*SpirEx*. §13, 15, 315), which edifies those who witness it. For all these reasons, Ignatius taught that it is appropriate for Christians to desire consolations (*SpirEx*. §6, 8, 319, 321), provided that they desire them for the above reasons (i.e., for the greater glory of God), and not simply for the sake of their enjoyment (*SpirEx*. §23, 152, 166–67, 179, 184; letter 466, trans. Palmer 255-256).

Unfortunately, writers are sharply divided on fundamental points regarding Ignatius's understanding of consolations. See Jules J. Toner, *A Commentary on Saint Ignatius' Rules for the Discernment of Spirits: A Guide to the Principles and Practice* (St. Louis, MO: Institute of Jesuit Sources, 1982), 81–144, and Brian O. McDermott, "Spiritual Consolation and Its Role in the Second Time of Election," *Studies in the Spirituality of Jesuits* 50, no. 4 (2018).

18. "Species that had been painted on it" alludes to the epistemology (theory of knowledge) of St. Thomas Aquinas (1225–74) that Ignatius had studied at the University of Paris. In essence, Ignatius was saying that even his capacity to understand the idea of unchastity had been taken from him. It is unlikely that he was indulging in hyperbole (see *Test.* §99), which would have been highly contrary to his customary and professed manner of speaking and writing (see Foreword of Gonçalves, n 7). Rather, he seems to be asserting that, during those few moments when the vision was happening, he was literally incapable of conceiving or entertaining unchastity in his mind. This interpretation falls easily within the range of mystical experiences reported by the saints.

19. In contrast, Laínez and Polanco asserted that Ignatius's gift of chastity resulted from a private vow of chastity that he had made in Aránzazu (Munitiz, *First Biographies*, 3–4, 43). That Ignatius did not mention this vow in the *Testament* was probably deliberate. In medieval theology, private vows—i.e., vows made to God without the witness or involvement of the church—were still binding under pain of mortal sin, and only approved ecclesiastical authorities could dispense Catholics from them. As superior general, Ignatius was ambivalent about Jesuits making private vows, as the duty to fulfill them could hinder Jesuits' availability for mission, or provoke anxieties and scruples. Laínez and Polanco both opined that Ignatius's vow was *zelus non secundum scientiam*, a medieval expression meaning pious but imprudent (Munitiz, *First Biographies*, 4, 43). Later, at the University of Paris, Ignatius's devout roommate Peter Faber suffered anxieties as a result of a private vow of chastity that he made when he was only twelve (see Murphy 62, 86, and Ch. 3, n 11).

20. The principal criterion for any discernment of spirits is whether a vision, idea, emotion, desire, etc., edifies oneself and others. Jesus taught that a tree is known by its fruit (Luke 6:43-45). Ignatius suggests that his newfound chastity was strong evidence in favor of his vision being truly from God, as opposed to a hallucination or a demonic deception. See *Life of St. Antony* §36; *SpirEx.* §316–17, 329.

21. The first of seven times that Ignatius refers to "persevering" (*perseverar*), see also *Test.* §15, 20, 21, 23, 25, 27). Here in §11, it appears in the same sentence with "resolutions" (*propósitos*), which also implied perseverance (see Ch. 1, n 24). When Ignatius was superior general,

the Society of Jesus was growing rapidly, but an unusually large number of men was also leaving, because they were not convinced that a life of service to others could save their souls as surely as long hours of prayer and fasting. Still others left because they wanted to return to their old lives of family and friends. The exodus was such that Pope Pius V (1504–72, r.1566–72) issued a letter in 1566 called *Aequum reputamus*, in which he forbade men to leave the Society for any reason, except if they wished to join a rigorous order of monks called the Carthusians (see Ch. 1, n 25). In this light, Ignatius would have wanted to use his *Testament* to underscore for Jesuit readers the need to persevere in their own vocations. Six times in the Jesuit *Constitutions*, he exhorts them "to live and die in the Society of Jesus" (§51, 119, 126, 193, 336, 511).

22. In the *Life of Christ*, Ludolph wrote: "The blessed virgin Cecilia was accustomed to read the life of Christ. [...] it is said that she always carried a copy of the gospels close to her heart. I understand this to mean that from the events of the life of Christ preserved in the gospels, she had chosen the ones that most moved her, and she meditated on these day and night with a pure and undivided heart [...] I encourage you to do the same. Of all the many kinds of spiritual exercise, I believe that this is the one that is the most necessary, the most beneficial, and the one that can lead you to the greatest heights" (trans. Walsh 1:10–11).

23. Comment by Gonçalves in the margins: "This had nearly three hundred pages, all written, quarto size" (*FontNarr*. 1:376).

24. The word *resolution* (*propósito* in Spanish, *proposito* in Italian) carried great weight in the theological jargon of sixteenth-century Catholicism. In the ancient church, Christians who made interior resolutions to serve God and the church in ways that were more ideal than what they were already doing were obliged to persevere in those commitments, even if they had made no formal promises or vows to that effect. The Latin word *propositum* denoted this resolution, from which derived the Spanish and Italian cognates. In the *Golden Legend*, the devil tries to tempt St. Francis "from his virtuous intention [*a salubris proposito*]" (trans. Ryan 2:220). In *Test*. §80, Ignatius notes that one of his early companions, Lope de Cáceres, abandoned Ignatius's way of life, and then began to behave in a manner that suggested he had "forgotten his first resolution [*primer propósito*]." See also Ch. 8, n 14. On

the *propositum* in the ancient and medieval church, including its use in early Jesuit documents, see Conwell, *Impelling Spirit*, 339–66.

25. Carthusians are an austere monastic order founded by St. Bruno of Cologne (*c.*1030–1101). They enjoyed a cordial relationship with Jesuits in the early decades of the Society's history, inspired partly by their high esteem for Faber (*FontNarr.* 1:753n2, *FontNarr.* 4:420–21, 426–31, *Epist.* 12:483–84). In 1547, Ignatius made a pact or "twinning agreement" (*hermanidad*) with them, whereby the graces merited by each order would benefit the other. In the bulls *Licet debitum* (October 18, 1549) and *Aequum reputamus* (January 17, 1566), popes declared Carthusians the only order for which men could leave the Society legitimately (*FontNarr.* 4:546–47).

26. Ignatius alludes to a famous story about Abba Pinufius. The elderly abba desired to escape the attention and temptations to pride that came with his reputation for holiness, and so he secretly fled to a distant monastery, "which he knew was stricter than all the others," and entered it anonymously. The monks treated him with disdain, thinking that he was a latecomer to the monastic vocation whose only motivation was food and shelter in his old age. Three years later, to Pinufius's disappointment, a monk discovered his real identity. See Cassian, *Institutes*, 4:30 (trans. Ramsey 94–96).

27. Comment by Gonçalves in the margins: "His brothers and others at home suspected he was planning some drastic change" (*FontNarr.* 1:378).

28. The image of Martín Loyola leading his brother from room to room in order to dissuade him from his new vocation alludes to Luke 4:5, where Satan shows Jesus all the kingdoms of the world in an attempt to lure him from the vocation he had only just begun (Luke 3:21–22). Ignatius, like Jesus, will face three temptations against his vocation. The next two are the "forceful thought" in *Test.* §20, and disgust with his religious vocation in *Test.* §25. As depicted in the *Testament*, Ignatius's three temptations were not to return to a life of sin per se, but to his previous life of family, friends, and service to his human king Ferdinand (1452–1516, r.1479–1516). While good in itself, it was not as ideal as the full commitment to Christ that he had just chosen. Thus, Martín tempts him with reminders of the duties and pleasures proper to family life. In a letter to Sr. Rejadell, Ignatius described his earlier temptations like so:

"How are you going to live your whole life amid such penance, with no enjoyment from friends, relatives, or possessions, leading such a lonely life and never having any ease? There are other less perilous ways you can save your soul" (letter 7, trans. Palmer 19). See *Life of St. Antony* §4, where the devil tempts Antony with memories of possessions, guardianship of his sister, bonds of kinship, love of money and glory, and the rigors of virtue. Bl. Raymond of Capua (1330–99) depicted the devil saying to St. Catherine of Siena (1347–80): "Be like other women, get yourself a husband and have children and increase the human race. If you want to please God, remember that even saints have married: think of Sara and Leah and Rachel. Why have you adopted this single life, which you cannot possibly keep up till the end?" (*The Life of St. Catherine of Siena*, trans. George Lamb [London: Harvill Press, 1960], 91). See also St. Francis in the *Golden Legend* (trans. Ryan 2:223).

29. "He slipped away" (*se descabulló* in Spanish). Shortly after Jesus began his mission, he was rejected by his friends and neighbors in Nazareth, and then "slipped away" from them (Luke 4:30).

2. Road to Montserrat (February to March 1522)

1. The brother was probably Pedro López Loyola, a parish priest. Seven years earlier, he and Ignatius were arraigned in court for "very enormous crimes." The records seem to indicate that they had ambushed and beaten a man during carnival time (*FontDoc.* 229–46).

2. In 1554, Ignatius wrote a letter to St. Francis Borgia in which he described the vigil (letter 4721, trans. Palmer 509–10).

3. Comment by Gonçalves in the margins: "From the day he left home, he always took the discipline each night" (*FontNarr.* 1:380). On the discipline, see Ch. 6, n 8.

4. The clause that "something happened to him that would be good to record" seems to imply that the story of the Moor was not already familiar to early Jesuits, and therefore required a brief apologetic for its inclusion in the *Testament*. Laínez and Polanco did not mention the Moor in their earlier lives of Ignatius.

5. In the *Conferences*, Cassian wrote that *discernment* (*discretio* in Latin, also commonly translated into English as *discretion*) is "light for the eye." Without it, a Christian "has not been fortified by true judgment and knowledge or has been deceived by some error or presumption."

Again without it, "it makes our whole body darkness—that is, it obscures all the clarity of our mind and also our actions, wrapping them in the blindness of vice and the darkness of confusion" (*Conferences* 2.2.5; trans. Ramsey 85–86).

6. Comment by Gonçalves in the margins: "He had such disgust for his past sins, and such a lively desire to do great things for the love of God, that though he made no judgment that his sins were forgiven, he did not give them much attention in the penances that he undertook to perform" (*FontNarr.* 1:382).

7. The desert fathers and mothers praised discretion as the most important of the monastic virtues, because it regulated all the rest. Cassian wrote: "And so, according to the opinion both of blessed Antony and of all the others, discretion was understood as that which would lead the fearless monk on a steady ascent to God and would always preserve the aforesaid virtues undamaged; as that with which the heights of perfection could be scaled with little weariness; and as that without which many of those who labor even with a good will would be unable to arrive at the summit. For discretion is the begetter, guardian, and moderator of all the virtues" (*Conferences* 2.4.1, trans. Ramsey 87).

8. "His whole intention" (*toda su intención*). A fundamental principle of Ignatius's mature spirituality is *pure intention*, meaning that when Christians are presented with two or more legitimate options in the service of God, they should be so motivated by love for God alone and for his glory, that they embrace or forego any option solely on the basis of what objectively serves his greater glory (*Cons.* §618). In other words, Christians should choose on the basis of what promises to edify the greater number of souls (the more *universal* good), as opposed to choosing on the basis of their personal desires and self-interests (a more *particular* good). Consequently, in *Test.* §14, Ignatius emphasizes that his new motivation is "to please and gratify God," and because "the saints had done so for the glory of God," and that he was not thinking of "any more particular consideration." Polanco wrote on Ignatius's behalf that "a very upright intention [*intención muy recta*]" means that Jesuits seek God's glory and the good of souls in every choice that they make, and while "always looking more to the universal than to the particular good" (letter 1848, trans. Palmer 338). See *Test.* §99.

Ignatius uses the expressions "pure intention," "right intention," and "simple intention" interchangeably in the above sense (e.g., *SpirEx.* §41, 46, 169; *Cons.* §135, 180, 288, 340, 360, 362, 813). Almost certainly, his inspiration was the *Imitation of Christ*, in which these expressions likewise are interchanged and serve as a leitmotif for the entire work (see esp. 2:4, 3:33). Thomas à Kempis's treatment of pure intention was itself a development of the classic Christian theme of "purity of heart" (*puritas cordis*) that Cassian and St. Augustine had developed in the context of the Sermon on the Mount: "Blessed are the pure of heart, for they shall see God" (Matt 5:8). See Juana Raasch, Harriet Luckman, and Linda Kulzer, eds., *Purity of Heart in Early Ascetic and Monastic Literature* (Collegeville, MN: Liturgical Press, 1999).

9.   *Moor* was a vague term to denote either a Muslim from the regions of North Africa, or a Muslim of dark complexion. In theory, Ferdinand and Isabella (1451–1504, r.1474–1504) had expelled all Muslims from Spain by 1492, and Ignatius's family had a history of fighting in battles against Muslims (*Chronicon* 1:516–17), so the conversation between Ignatius and the Moor was probably tense from the start.

10. The Quran affirms the virgin birth of Jesus, but it does not address Mary's perpetual virginity.

11. In many cultures, an intact hymen is erroneously believed to be proof of a woman's virginity, and even the essence itself of female virginity. The Moor was arguing that Mary's hymen would have broken when she gave birth to Jesus, so that effectively she was no longer a virgin. Ignatius was startled and embarrassed to find himself defending his Lady on so intimate a matter, which led to his subsequent anger.

12. Modern commentators sometimes explain this story in terms of Ignatius feeling impulses to violence and intolerance, and his nascent realization that killing people for their religious beliefs is wrong. As attractive as that interpretation is, one must allow Ignatius to be a man of his time. The story is clear that he would have killed the Moor had the mule taken the road to town, indicating that violence remained a legitimate option in his mind. Years later, as superior general, Ignatius obtained a papal indulgence for Catholics fighting Islamic forces in North Africa (letter 1267, trans. Palmer 316–17). *Test.* §14 is explicit that the story of the Moor was included to convey how God had protected Ignatius from his ignorance of

discernment. It also symbolizes his victory over anger, one of eight deadly temptations elaborated by Cassian, all of which Ignatius will face on his way to Jerusalem. In the *Conferences*, Cassian links anger to a lack of discernment (2:4, trans. Ramsey 86).

13. Comment by Gonçalves in the margins: "He also bought some slippers, but kept just one. He did not do this for the sake of style. He had one leg all tied up with a bandage, and it was somewhat neglected. Each night he found it swollen, even though he had been riding [on a mule all day]. He thought that this foot should have a shoe" (*Font-Narr.* 1:384, 386).

14. Amadís of Gaul was a mythical prince of a fictional region in Brittany. His tales of chivalry, comprising four volumes by one or more unknown authors, were popular two hundred years before Ignatius. Garci Rodríguez de Montalvo (1450–1504) wrote a four-volume revised version that enjoyed an incredible thirty editions. He then wrote a sequel about Amadís's son Esplandián, who made a vigil of arms before an image of the Virgin Mary. For an English translation of Montalvo's first four volumes, see *Amadís of Gaul*, trans. Edwin Place and Herbert Behm (Lexington, KY: University Press of Kentucky, 2003).

15. A Christian vigil in general is the practice of remaining awake and silent throughout the night, in a church or shrine, to pray, reflect, and contemplate a sacred object such as a painting, statue, or tomb. In *Test.* §13, Ignatius kept vigil before a retablo of *Nuestra Señora de Aránzazu*, patroness of Guipúzcoa; he kept vigil again in *Test.* §18. A *vigil of arms*, more specifically, was a medieval custom that took place the night before a squire was dubbed a knight. He bathed, fasted, made a confession, and then spent the night contemplating his weapons, his new duties before God, and his willingness to fight and die for his king and queen.

16. A general confession was an optional practice, popular among Catholics at this time, of confessing all the sins of one's life that one could remember, as opposed to confessing only those sins that one had committed since one's last confession. On the benefits of general confessions, see *SpirEx.* §44.

17. The dagger was soon lost to history. The sword remained in the monastery for many years, after which the Benedictines donated it to the Society of Jesus. It is on display in the Església del Sagrat Cor de Jesus (Church of the Sacred Heart of Jesus) in Barcelona.

18. The confessor Fr. Jean Chanon showed Ignatius the *Ejercitatorio de la vida espiritual* (Book of Exercises for the Spiritual Life) by Fr. García Jiménez de Cisneros (1455–1510), an abbot of the monastery who had died ten years before Ignatius's arrival. The book likely inspired Ignatius to write his own spiritual exercises, and perhaps more specifically, parts of the First Week and "Examinations of Conscience." But in general, the contents of the books are quite different. The most recent English translation appears to be E. Allison Peers (*Book of Exercises for the Spiritual Life* [Montserrat: Monastery of Montserrat, 1929]). See Terence O'Reilly, "The *Exercises* of Saint Ignatius Loyola and the *Exercitatorio de la vida espiritual*," *Studia monastica* 16, no. 2 (1974): 301–23.

19. Conversions of nobles and the wealthy to Christianity, or to a more fervent practice of it, exerted a special fascination on ancient and medieval Christians, as exemplified by stories in the *Golden Legend* about St. Agatha (*c.*231–*c.*251), St. Perpetua (*fl.* third century), and St. Francis of Assisi. As the youngest child of a noble family, Ignatius did not stand to inherit land or wealth, but he was nevertheless a *hidalgo*, meaning a Spanish nobleman who was, in modern terms, "famous for being famous" (see Ch. 4, n 4). As such, the Catholic faithful would have recognized his conversion as following in this storied tradition. In Manresa, a young Juan Pascual and his friends repeatedly asked Ignatius why he led a life of humility and anonymity when he was a knight and came from a leading noble family (*Scripta* 2:640).

20. Ignatius had planned to rest in Manresa only a few days, but he ended by staying eleven months, from March 1522 to February 1523. Scholars debate the reason(s) for this unexpected sojourn. A popular myth holds that Ignatius lived in a cave just outside the city. Ignatius never mentioned a cave. He seems to have divided his stay between the hospice and the homes of various benefactors such as the Pascual and Amigant families. But it is likely that Ignatius visited the cave to pray and to write notes for what later became the *Spiritual Exercises*. With regard to Ignatius staying at a "hospice," see Ch. 6, n 25.

21. *Test.* §18 ends with the first of seventeen *et ceteras*. In the sixteenth century, Spanish writers often used these to indicate that readers would or should be able to fill in the rest of the details on their own.

3. Sojourn at Manresa (March 1522 to February 1523)

1. The Latin phrase *agere contra*, meaning "to act against," denotes a basic
   strategy in ancient and medieval spiritual literature. It is not enough
   simply to resist temptations, in which case they inevitably return and
   wear a person down over time. One eliminates them altogether, or at
   least weakens them, by counter-attacking, i.e., by acting in a manner
   directly opposed to them. For example, if one is tempted to skip Mass
   on Sundays, one might go twice a week until the temptation leaves.
   In particular, the desert fathers and mothers taught disciples that
   any temptations to hide sinful or embarrassing thoughts from their
   teachers should be assaulted with full transparency: "Today you have
   triumphed over your conqueror and adversary, defeating him by your
   confession more decisively than you yourself had been overthrown by
   him because of your silence [...] And therefore, after he has been dis-
   closed, the most wicked spirit will no longer be able to disturb you,
   nor shall the filthy serpent ever again seize a place to make his lair in
   you, now that by a salutary confession he has been drawn out from the
   darkness of your heart into the light" (Cassian, *Conferences* 2:11, trans.
   Ramsey 92; see also *SpirEx*. §326). *Agere contra* was a favorite strategy
   of Ignatius (see *Test*. §32, 52, 55, 82, 83; *SpirEx*. §13, 319–21, 324–26,
   351). In *Test*. §19, he dishevels his appearance to counter-attack his
   vanity. One particular form of *agere contra* is "talking back" to temptations, instead of ignoring them or passively resisting them (see *Test*.
   §20 and Ch. 3, n 5).

2. Note the similarity with *Test*. §8, where Ignatius is attracted to the possibility of returning to his old life, but when he finishes daydreaming
   about it, he is left feeling dry and restless. Thus, his remark here about
   the vision of the serpent, that "when it disappeared, he was displeased,"
   foreshadows that it is not divine in origin.

3. The shift to the plural—"as if they were saying" (*como que si dijeran*)—
   probably implies the influence of demons behind the thought.

4. Early Jesuits often used the words "life" or "this life" to denote their particular way of serving God. In the *Testament*, the words appear about
   ten times to mean Ignatius's way of serving God (e.g., §20, 21, 25, 64,
   70, 74). Diego Hoces (*c*.1490–1538), for example, made up his mind "to
   imitate the pilgrim's life" (§92, *seguitare la vita del peregrino*). This consideration sheds light on how to interpret Ignatius's cure from scruples

in *Test.* §25, an otherwise obscure passage (see Ch. 3, n 15). Today, the Society prefers to use the phrase "our way of proceeding," which also goes back to the early Jesuits.

5. Ignatius employs a popular tactic of desert spirituality called *antirrhêtikos*, or "talking back" to one's fears and temptations. When demons tried to frighten St. Antony with raucous animal noises, he shouted back to them, "If there were some power among you, it would have been enough for only one of you to come. But since the Lord has broken your strength, you attempt to terrify me by any means with the mob [...] If you are able, and you did receive authority over me, don't hold back, but attack. But if you are unable, why, when it is vain, do you disturb me?" (trans. Gregg 39). Ignatius advised Sr. Rejadell to use this technique against her own troubling thoughts (letter 7, trans. Palmer 18–20). The benefits of this practice remain valid regardless of whether one understands demons metaphorically or literally. Modern psychologists often recommend it to people with eating disorders. See David Brakke, *Evagrius of Pontus: Talking Back—Antirrhêtikos—A Monastic Handbook for Combating Demons* (Collegeville, MN: Liturgical Press, 2009). For a dramatic example of Ignatius practicing this technique, see ch 6, n 9. See also *Imitation of Christ* 3:6; St. Teresa's *Book of Her Life* 25.

6. "After what is mentioned above" refers to Martín trying to dissuade Ignatius from his new life (*Test.* §12). It is significant that Gonçalves draws attention to the manner in which he depicts the temptations (see Ch. 1, n 28). They span the gamut of Ignatius's *past* sins (scruples), *present* familial duties (the temptations by Martín Loyola), and *future* perseverance (the forceful thought). In the *Spiritual Exercises*, Ignatius juxtaposes past, present, and future considerations for making an election and persevering in it (e.g., §187, 323).

7. Cassian asked Abba Daniel why monks one minute could be "so filled with gladness of heart and a kind of unspeakable joy and abundance of holy sentiments," and then the next minute, "why, with no apparent cause, would we so suddenly be filled with anguish and oppressed with a certain irrational sadness." The abba replied, "Three reasons have been handed down by our forebears for this mental barrenness of which you speak. It comes either from our own negligence or from an attack of the devil or as the Lord's design and trial" (*Conferences* 4.2, trans. Ramsey 155–56). See also *SpirEx.* §322, 335.

8.   *Beatas* were Spanish laywomen renowned for their holiness, charitable works, and mystical prophecies. The Catholic faithful gave them mixed reactions. Bishops and royalty often consulted them, while others denounced them as heretics and frauds. Scholars debate the identity of this particular *beata*.

9.   Cassian used the expression "soldier of Christ" (*miles Christi*) throughout the *Institutes* and *Conferences*, always with reference to monks, as opposed to Christians in general. In *Institutes* 10:3, he cited 2 Tim. 2:4 to describe the effects of acedia, that "the soldier of Christ, having become a fugitive and deserter from [God's] army, 'entangles himself in worldly affairs' and displeases 'him to whom he engaged himself'" (trans. Ramsey 220–21). Cassian followed this with a description of acedia as "sleep" (*Institutes* 10:4–5). In that light, it is probably not coincidental that the account of Ignatius's scruples and (implied) acedia that bring him to the brink of abandoning his vocation (*Test.* §22–25) is prefaced with a reference to him as a soldier of Christ, and concludes with the observation that he awakened "as if from sleep." See Ch. 3, n 16.

10.   Scruples properly so-called do not mean a person's close attention to "little" sins and temptations, which in fact is necessary to grow in the spiritual life (*SpirEx.* §32–43, 345–49; letter 7, trans. Palmer 20-21). Rather, scruples are a nagging uncertainty whether one has sinned in a particular situation, a malady that is more common in one who is attentive to little sins and temptations (see *Test.* §36). At one level, Ignatius knew that his confessor was right: that he had not sinned by forgetting to mention some sins during confession. But he still felt a nagging fear that he had offended God. Initially, he believed that God was sending him the desire to make a perfect confession for the sake of his spiritual growth, but later he realizes that it is a disguised temptation from the devil (*Test.* §25). Ignatius's advice in the *Spiritual Exercises* regarding scruples (§351) seems to be taken from a story about St. Bernard (1090–1153) in the *Golden Legend* (trans. Ryan 2:103–4).

11.   In the sixteenth century, Catholics frequently anguished over the possibility that they had made incomplete or insincere confessions, the young monk Martin Luther (1483–1546) being a famous example. Faber wrote in his diary: "[My scruples at the University of Paris] were over the fear that over a long period I had not properly confessed

my sins, which gave me so much anxiety that to get a remedy I would gladly have gone to a desert to eat herbs and roots forever" (trans. Murphy 65).

12. Ignatius repeatedly consulted others about his scruples and (implied) acedia, with no success. Gonçalves possibly intended an allusion to Cassian's *Institutes* 10:25: "When I was starting to dwell in the desert and had told Abba Moses, the highest of all the holy ones, that the previous day I had been very seriously troubled by the malady of acedia and that I had been unable to free myself from it except by running at once to Abba Paul, he said: 'You did not free yourself from it; instead, you surrendered and subjected yourself to it all the more. For the adversary will fight you even more strenuously as soon as he sees that you are a deserter and a fugitive and that you have fled defeated from the conflict, unless you join in the fray once again and learn to triumph by endurance and by doing battle instead of choosing to dissipate its passions, when they assail you, by deserting your cell or by torpid sleep.' Hence experience proves that an onslaught of acedia must not be avoided by flight but overcome through resistance" (trans. Ramsey 234). See Ch. 3, n. 15 and 16.

13. The Spanish reads that Ignatius wanted to jump from a large *agujero*, meaning "hole." While a large hole in Ignatius's bedroom is possible, it seems odd. Perhaps Gonçalves's scribe meant to write *aguja*, meaning the top of an obelisk-shaped tower. Symbolically, this would link Ignatius's anguish perfectly with Jesus's third temptation, where Satan leads him to the top of the Jewish temple, saying, "If you are the Son of God, throw yourself down from here" (Luke 4:9; see Ch. 1, n 28). If one prefers the first interpretation, it still presupposes that the bedroom was high off the ground. The monastery no longer exists, but a Dominican tradition holds that Ignatius stayed on the first floor (*A Pilgrim's Journey: The Autobiography of Ignatius of Loyola*, trans. Joseph N. Tylenda [San Francisco: Ignatius Press, 2001], 71n10). The conundrum is resolved if one accepts that Ignatius and/or Gonçalves indulged in literary license for the sake of the biblical allusion.

14. Polanco noted that Ignatius got this idea after reading "the lives of the fathers," meaning the desert fathers (*Chronicon* 1:21). This would make the saint in question Abba James of the Cells. Being "a simple man" who had not studied theology, James became confused and distressed

when both Orthodox and Monophysite Christians urged him to join their ranks. He did not know which side taught the truth about Jesus, so he fasted for forty days, and even wore burial clothes in preparation for his death, until an angel appeared to him and told him to join the Orthodox (see Ward, *Sayings of the Desert Fathers*, 240–41).

15.   "Disgust for the life he led" does not refer to Ignatius's scruples per se—something for which he already felt disgust for many months—but to his religious vocation in general (see Ch. 3, n 4). That is, when scruples finally succeeded in making him feel revulsion for his commitment to follow Christ unreservedly, so that he had desires to return to his old life, it was then that he realized that his impulse to make a perfect confession was not from God, but from the enemy. Implicit here is a key principle of medieval spirituality about the necessity of always going *from good to better* in the divine service (e.g., *SpirEx.* §315, 331, 335), so that any thoughts of going back to a less-ideal form of life are recognizable *ipso facto* as temptations from the enemy. Ignatius later wrote: "[Jesuits] would not dare to turn back from a more perfect to a less perfect manner of proceeding. Rather, it is our fervent wish for his own greater service and praise, God our Lord would take us from this life rather than let us set such an example for those who are to come" (letter 109, trans. Palmer 127). See also *Life of St. Antony* §3–5; *Life of Jesus Christ* 14 (trans. Walsh 1:289); and Faber's *Memoriale* (trans. Murphy 328–29).

16.   Gonçalves alludes to a kind of spiritual depression called *acedia*, also known as "the noonday demon" in the desert tradition. Cassian wrote that it causes monks to feel "disgust of the heart" (*tædium cordis*) for monastic life, with temptations to leave it, or barring that, monks fall into a "sleep" (*somnus*) in which they go through the motions of monastic life while in unconscious despair (*Institutes* 10:3–6). Ultimately, acedia can lead to thoughts of suicide. Faber wrote of it that a person "despairs of success and is driven, full of disgust and sadness, to take refuge in flight. Further, he is easily deceived, is ready to judge whatever happens as for the worst, and quickly becomes filled with suspicion" (trans. Murphy 169). See also *Imitation of Christ* 4:10; Jean-Charles Nault, *The Noonday Devil: Acedia, the Unnamed Evil of Our Times*, trans. Michael J. Miller (San Francisco: Ignatius Press, 2015); Kathleen Norris, *Acedia & Me: A Marriage, Monks, and a Writer's Life* (New York: Riverhead Books, 2008).

17. See *SpirEx.* §333–34. Laínez and Polanco made only brief reference to Ignatius's scruples, and they wrote nothing about him contemplating suicide. It suggests that Ignatius and/or Gonçalves emphasized the story in order to illustrate the dangers of scruples. As superior general, Ignatius often had to write letters of advice to people who suffered from it. See *Cons.* §48, 136, 235, 330, 559; Eaglestone §135, 272, 276, 294–95, 305, 356; letter 7 (trans. Palmer 18–22), and letter 6615 (trans. Palmer 688–89).

18. Spiritual masters on the Iberian Peninsula such as Luís de Granada (1504–88) and St. Pedro de Alcántara (1499–1562) promoted the idea that sixty to ninety minutes of contemplative prayer a day were necessary to prepare for mystical union, should God deign to grant it. Others went much further, insisting on four to six hours. Immediately after his conversion, Ignatius shared that mentality, but his later focus on service to others resulted in a sharp decrease in the time that he allotted to formal prayer. As superior general, he resisted pressures from Jesuits who wanted a more monastic lifestyle. Thus, in the *Constitutions*, Ignatius's treatment of Jesuit prayer downplays the traditional monastic goal of infused union in favor of *pure intention*, meaning Jesuits' efforts to make the greater glory of God the criterion for all their discernments, and *devotion*, meaning the ease, alacrity, and heartfelt affection with which Jesuits enter into this particular form of active contemplation (*Test.* §99).

19. In *Life of St. Antony* §51–52, spiritual thoughts distract Antony from sleep and study. Gerson wrote in *Snares of the Devil*: "Sometimes the devil gives a man a fund of useful thoughts, but at the wrong time, and simply to hinder prayer. For he sends these thoughts for a bad end, and so at a very unsuitable time" (3:7). See Ch. 6, n 2.

20. Apparently an example of the "First Time of Election" in *SpirEx.* §175, which "is when God Our Lord so moves and attracts the will that without doubting or being able to doubt, such a dedicated soul follows what is shown." Writers debate what Ignatius meant by the "first time." In the opinion of this editor, one briefly experiences a form of infused contemplation, so that one is incapable of doubting while it happens, even if one wished to do so as a hypothetical exercise; and since this is a gratuitous gift from God, so that a person is incapable of approximating it through effort, it often is perceived as

occurring out of the blue (i.e., as having no thematic connection to the thoughts and feelings immediately preceding the onset of the experience). Ignatius seems to describe something like this in a letter to Sr. Rejadell: "It often happens that our Lord moves and drives our soul to one action or another by opening the soul up, that is, by speaking inside it without the din of words [i.e., infused contemplation], lifting the soul wholly to his divine love, so that even if we wished to resist his impression, we could not" (letter 7, trans. Palmer 21). However, Ignatius added that, in the emotional afterglow of the experience, the enemy can insinuate deceits. St. Teresa of Ávila makes similar distinctions in *The Book of Her Life* 25 (trans. Kavanaugh 212–23). See also *SpirEx.* §330.

21.   In the twentieth century, writers made much of Ignatius's supposedly novel emphasis on God teaching through personal experience. In fact, the idea is prominent in scripture (e.g., Isaiah 54:13, Job 6:45, Jeremiah 31:34, 1 Thess. 4:9, 1 John 2:27), the desert tradition, and medieval literature. St. Athanasius wrote in the *Life of St. Antony*, "Again, [Antony] had this favor from God. When he sat alone on the mountain, if ever in his reflections he failed to find a solution, it was revealed to him by Providence in answer to his prayer: the happy man was, in the words of Scripture, *taught of God*" (§66). In the *Golden Legend*, when someone asked St. Dominic which book he studied the most, he replied "the book of love" (trans. Ryan 2:53). St. Bernard "confessed that whatever he knew about the Scriptures he had learned while meditating and praying in the woods and the fields, and he sometimes said among his friends he had no teachers except the oaks and the beeches" (trans. Ryan 2:101). See Ch. 7, n 1.

22.   Laínez seems to imply, and Polanco explicitly affirms, that Ignatius's bouts with scruples came *after* his mystical illumination at the Cardoner. Polanco added that God sent the scruples for his "purity of soul," that is, to protect Ignatius from sinful pride as a result of the illumination (Munitiz, *First Biographies*, 6, 46). Notably, Ignatius and/or Gonçalves reversed the order in the *Testament*, probably to reflect the traditional theology of the illuminative way following the purgative way. Ignatius refers to these ways in *SpirEx.* §10.

23.   Nadal wrote that one of Ignatius's most extraordinary mystical gifts was the ability to distinguish which Person of the Trinity was

communicating with him in prayer (*Nadal* 4:651). This is clear from the surviving pages of Ignatius's so-called Spiritual Diary (*Ignatius of Loyola: Personal Writings; Reminiscences, Spiritual Diary, Select Letters Including the Text of the* Spiritual Exercises, trans. Joseph A. Munitiz and Philip Endean [London: Penguin, 1996], 67–109).

24. Laínez reported that Ignatius had said the same to him (Munitiz, *First Biographies*, 8). Many if not most of the desert fathers and mothers were illiterate, and few had access to a copy of the scriptures. For that reason, they relied heavily on memorization of passages. Yet they distinguished between hermits who merely memorized the scriptures and those who embodied the scriptures in lived practice. At a time when heresies and fears of heresy were rife, many abbas and ammas were reluctant to attempt to articulate an authoritative interpretation of the scriptures, preferring instead to speak of their own experience. See Ward, *Sayings of the Desert Fathers*, 18–19, 31–32, 167, 182–83, 197.

25. Comment by Gonçalves in the margins: "This left his understanding so very enlightened that he felt as if he were another man with another mind" (*FontNarr.* 1:404, 406). Ignatius does not go into detail about his mystical illumination. Years later, after the founding of the Society, he justified the Society's novel ways of proceeding on the basis of "something that happened to me at Manresa" (Eaglestone §137). One might deduce, therefore, from his characteristic emphases on apostolic service, the more universal good, "seeking God in all things," and using all legitimate human means in the service of God, that his illumination transformed his perception of God's relationship to creation. God does not create the world and then watch it from a distance, intervening in human affairs as necessary. Rather, God is intimately present and active in every person and place. He sustains creation in existence at every moment, and he "labors" at every moment to draw good from every human choice and historical event. In this sense, God can invite the baptized to labor with him in his one act of sanctifying the world. This has thematic ties to Ignatius's later mystical experience at La Storta (*Test.* §96). See Charles J. Jackson, "'Something That Happened to Me at Manresa': The Mystical Origin of the Ignatian Charism," *Studies in the Spirituality of Jesuits* 38, no. 2 (2006).

26. Jacobus wrote of St. Francis in the *Golden Legend*: "He preferred to hear himself reviled rather than praised, and when people extolled the

merits of his sanctity, he ordered one of the friars to assail his ears with abuse epithets. The friar, all unwilling, called him a bumpkin, a money-lover, an ignoramus, and a worthless fellow, and Francis cheered and said: 'Lord bless you, brother! You have told the truth, and I need to hear such things!'" (trans. Ryan 2:226).

27. "Embarrassment and sorrow" for not having used his gifts well (i.e., contrary to pride). Cassian elaborated a list of eight deadly thoughts that monks must resist in their quest for purity of heart (see *Institutes* 5–12, trans. Ramsey 113–279; *Conferences* 5, trans. Ramsey 177–209) that the later Catholic tradition reduced to the famous "seven deadly sins" known today. In the *Testament*, Gonçalves alludes subtly to all eight temptations, and in almost the same order that Cassian listed them: gluttony (§19), lust (§10), greed (§13), anger (§15), sadness (§21), acedia (§25), vainglory (§32), and pride (§33).

28. Due to extreme fasting in the initial years of his spiritual journey, Ignatius suffered agonizing stomach pains for the rest of his life. When he was superior general, the pain left him bedridden for days and weeks. After his death, Dr. Realdo Colombo (*c.*1515–59) reported that, during the autopsy, he had removed "nearly countless [*innumerabiles pene*]" gallstones from the kidneys, lungs, liver, and portal vein (*FontNarr.* 1:769n16). Consequently, self-care was a prominent theme in Ignatius's letters to Jesuits. They needed to eat properly, get enough sleep, and take a vacation or retreat annually, provided of course that they continued to practice an appropriate asceticism and to respect their vow of poverty. Longer, healthier lives would enable Jesuits to serve a greater number of souls. See Barton T. Geger, "*Cura personalis*: Some Ignatian Inspirations," *Jesuit Higher Education* 3, no. 2 (January 2014).

29. Catholics were required to obtain permission from the pope for pilgrimages to the Holy Land. He granted these only on Easter Day, which is one possible reason why Ignatius prolonged his stay in Manresa unexpectedly.

30. Ignatius frequently refers to seeking the counsel of holy persons (e.g., *Test.* §21–23, 36–37). The scriptures often commended this practice (e.g., Proverbs 12:15, 13:10, Wisdom 6:24–25, 1 Kings 1:12, Tobit 4:18), and it was central to the spirituality of the desert tradition. "If [Antony] heard of a zealous person anywhere, he searched him out like the wise bee. He

did not go back to his own place until he had seen him, and as though receiving from him certain supplies for travelling the road to virtue, he returned" (*Life of St. Antony* §3, trans. Gregg 32). The entirety of Cassian's *Conferences* is predicated upon this practice (see appendix 2:2–4); see also *Imitation of Christ* 1:8; *Snares of the Devil* 1:7. Gerson further observed that some Christians consulted holy persons for the sake of appearances or to placate their own bad consciences (*Snares* 1:6, 3:5).

4. Pilgrimage to Jerusalem (March to September 1523)

1. *Con una hija que traía en hábitos de muchacho.* Laymen and laywomen commonly wore the religious garb of monks or mendicants while on pilgrimage; for women, this had the added benefit of disguising their gender, reducing the likelihood of assault. The Spanish is unclear whether the mother dressed her daughter like a boy, or dressed her in a religious habit. English traveler Fynes Moryson (1566–1630) described seeing women on pilgrimage in religious habits in *An Itinerary*, 4 vols. (London, 1617), 1:308, 4:222.

2. In his petition, Ignatius identified himself as a minor cleric of the diocese of Pamplona (*FontDoc.* 289–90), meaning that he had been tonsured earlier, probably at age seven. Years earlier, he had identified himself as a cleric to evade the jurisdiction of civil courts for "very enormous crimes" (*FontDoc.* 229–46). These and other factors make it somewhat misleading to call Ignatius a "layman" in the years before his ordination to the diaconate and priesthood, regardless of whether one understands that term in letter or in spirit. See Barton T. Geger, "Ten Things That St. Ignatius Never Said or Did," *Studies in the Spirituality of Jesuits* 50, no. 1 (2018): 24–26.

3. "As we have mentioned above" (*como arriba hemos dicho*), see *Test.* §29. This appears to be the only use of "we" to refer to the narrator of the *Testament.* It might be a simple literary indulgence, but perhaps it is a conscious acknowledgment of the dual contributions of Ignatius and Gonçalves.

4. Ignatius had sufficient name-recognition to expect assistance from the imperial ambassador, had he chosen to avail himself of that help. It suggests that he was not as obscure during his so-called pilgrim years as many writers seem to presuppose. See *Test.* §63, where Ignatius goes over the heads of the inquisitors by appealing his case directly to the

archbishop.

5.   In 1546, Ignatius wrote similar advice to Jesuits attending the Council
      of Trent, where they could expect tense conversations between church-
      men, some of whom would have been sympathetic to the Protestant
      reforms (letter 123, trans. Palmer 128–31).

6.   The ship was called the *Negrona*. It left Venice on July 14, 1523. Two
      passengers wrote detailed accounts of their passage and sojourn in the
      Holy Land: Peter Füssli of Zurich (1482–1548), in *Zürcher Taschenbuch*
      7 (1884): 146–93, and Philip Hagan of Strasbourg, in *Vier Rheinische
      Palaestina-Pilgerschriften Des XIV, XV, und XVI Jahrhunderts*, ed. Lud-
      wig Conrady (Wiesbaden, 1882), 230–89. Neither mentions Ignatius.
      For a detailed account of a friar's two pilgrimages to Jerusalem in 1480
      and 1483, see H. F. M. [Hilda Frances Margaret] Prescott, *Friar Felix at
      Large: A Fifteenth-Century Pilgrimage to the Holy Land* (New Haven:
      Yale University Press, 1950).

7.   The sailors were engaging in sexual acts in front of the passengers.
      According to Ribadeneira, Ignatius rebuked them "fully, freely, and
      continuously" (trans. Pavur 43). Other Spanish passengers attempted
      unsuccessfully to quiet him for fear that the sailors would harm him.

8.   The pilgrims arrived on September 4, 1523. On the fifth, they saw
      Mount Zion, the Cenacle, and Holy Sepulcher; on the sixth, the Way
      of the Cross, on the seventh, Bethany and the Mount of Olives, on the
      eighth and ninth, Bethlehem, on the tenth, Josaphat and Cedron, and
      on the eleventh, a return to the Holy Sepulcher. They rested the next
      two days. On the fourteenth, they went to Jericho and the Jordan River,
      and then they remained in Jerusalem until their departure on the
      twenty-third.

9.   Popes had entrusted members of the Franciscan order to care for the
      Christian holy sites in Jerusalem. "Guardian" was the title of the supe-
      rior of the Franciscan house.

10.   Ignatius desired to convert Muslims to Christianity and thereby to
      become a martyr (*FontNarr.* 2:33). Muslims had ruled Jerusalem
      intermittently ever since they first conquered it in the year 638. In
      Ignatius's day, they permitted Christian pilgrims to visit, but they
      threatened to execute anyone who tried to convert them. In such an
      eventuality, the lives of the Franciscans, who were responsible for the
      pilgrims, also would be at risk. Naturally, this made the Franciscans

skittish of zealous pilgrims, for which reason Ignatius is not fully transparent about his motives for being there. Ironically, years later, as superior general, Ignatius had to invoke his own authority when denying the requests of Borgia and other Jesuits to be martyrs in Jerusalem (letter 4182, trans. Palmer 470–71). See Emanuele Colombo, "Defeating the Infidels, Helping Their Souls: Ignatius Loyola and Islam," in *A Companion to Ignatius of Loyola: Life, Writings, Spirituality, Influence*, ed. Robert Maryks (Leiden: Brill, 2014), 179–97. What Athanasius wrote in the *Life of St. Antony* (§46) applies equally to Ignatius: "[Antony] grieved because he had not been martyred, but the Lord was protecting him to benefit us and others, so that he might be a teacher to many in the discipline [spiritual exercises] that he had learned from the Scriptures. For simply by seeing his conduct, many aspired to become imitators of his way of life" (trans. Gregg 66).

11. Ignatius sent a letter to Juan Pascual, age sixteen, son of Inés Pascual, a principal benefactor in Manresa. A year earlier, they had given Ignatius a bedroom in their home, and Juan was devoted to the pilgrim ever since. During Ignatius's studies in Barcelona, Juan asked to be his follower. Ignatius refused, probably because Juan was the only son of a widow. Many years later, as the grandfather of seventy-seven, Juan loved to regale family and friends with stories of Ignatius's stay with them. Ignatius's letter to Juan has been lost, but Ribadeneira had access to it when he wrote his *Life of Ignatius*. Ribadeneira refers to it explicitly (book 1, chapter 2, trans. Pavur 44), and he seems to have copied its content when relating Ignatius's activities from the time he left Venice to the time he left Jerusalem.

12. As superior general, Ignatius had to address the problem of Muslim pirates who kidnapped Jesuits for ransom (letter 5544, trans. Palmer 84–89).

13. Syrian Christians who served in the monastery were called "belted" (*cristianos de la cintura*) because of their style of dress.

5. Return to Spain (October 1523 to February 1524)

1. In the *Golden Legend*, St. Dominic asks a boatman to ferry him across a river despite not having any money. The boatman demands Dominic's cape as payment. Dominic prays briefly, then finds a coin on the ground by his feet (Ryan 2:51).

2. According to legend, the apostle St. James the Greater sailed to Spain to preach the Gospel. A church in Muxía, Galicia, marks the spot of his landing. He later returned to Jerusalem, where he was the first of the twelve apostles to be martyred (Acts of the Apostles 12:2). James's disciples carried his body back to Spain, where the bishop Theodemar of Iria (d.847) rediscovered it about the year 830. The apostle's remains now rest in the cathedral of Santiago de Compostela. Over the centuries, his tomb became the most popular destination in Europe for Christian pilgrims. To this day, thousands of pilgrims hike the *Camino de Santiago* annually.

3. The threat of excommunication is what changed Ignatius's mind. If following his own inner conviction about God's will meant separation from the mystical body of the church, then he was obliged to conclude that his conviction was mistaken. This was one fundamental difference between Ignatius and the Illuminati with whom he was often confused. On the Illuminati, see Ch. 6, n 12.

4. "What ought to be done" (*quid agendum*). Here, Ignatius and/or Gonçalves used a Latin expression that appears nowhere else in the text. Until this point in the *Testament*, Ignatius often had asked himself what he should do, but always in Spanish, suggesting that this particular decision was different from the others. *Quid agendum* has no agent implied (i.e., it does not mean what *he* ought, but what *anyone* ought in that situation). Since Ignatius had just affirmed in the first half of the sentence that his subjective convictions about God's will had been mistaken, he perhaps puts his new discernment in more philosophical, universal terms, to imply a criterion more objective, less subjective, namely that which serves the more universal good. See Gonçalves' Foreword, no 3, and Ch. 2, no 8.

5. Apparently, on his return voyage, Ignatius decided to become a priest, since there would have been little reason otherwise to study theology in the sixteenth century. Surprisingly, he makes no mention in his *Testament* of this momentous decision. To explain the silence, some

writers have conjectured that Ignatius preferred to remain an itinerant layman, but after his expulsion from Jerusalem, he chose priesthood for the practical benefit of church authorities taking him more seriously. Yet this interpretation is doubtful, given that Ignatius is silent in the *Testament* about numerous pivotal moments in his life, and that he later made the Society an order of *clerks regular*, meaning an order composed essentially of priests, as opposed to a lay congregation, or to a so-called "mixed order" of priests and laymen.

6.	A belief possibly inspired by Matt. 23:8–10. Spanish has different forms of the singular pronoun *you*, one to address persons of authority, the other for family and friends. In the sixteenth century, these pronouns were evolving rapidly, but in general they were *Vuestra merced* and *Vos*, respectively. Today in Spain, they are *Usted* and *Tú*. Old English had distinguished between *You* and *Thou*, but the latter fell into disuse in the seventeenth century.

7.	Andrea Doria of the Republic of Genoa (1466–1560) was an admiral of a fleet in the service of King Francis I of France (1494–1547, r.1515–47).

6. Barcelona and Alcalá (February 1524 to June 1527)

1.	Isabella Roser was the wife of a wealthy cloth merchant. She met Ignatius in late February or early March of the previous year (1523), when he was passing through Barcelona on his way to Jerusalem. After he returned to Barcelona, she recruited other wealthy women, spiritual devotees of Ignatius, to finance his studies and sustenance. This "Ignatian circle" continued to exist for several decades. In 1540, when Ignatius was superior general in Rome, he missioned two Jesuits to Barcelona, who themselves became close friends with these women. In 1541, Roser's husband died, and she conceived the idea of going to Rome to start a congregation of women under obedience to Ignatius. He was firmly opposed to the idea, but Roser made her case to the pope, who ordered Ignatius to receive her vows and those of two other women. Roser then donated the remainder of her estate to the Society. Ignatius assigned the women to work with reformed prostitutes at the House of St. Martha. But Roser's behavior was highly problematic, including spending the Society's funds without Ignatius's approval. Nine months later, the pope permitted Ignatius to release the women from their vows. Roser then sued the Society for the return of her money, goaded by two nephews who were angry about their lost inheritance. She lost the suit, after Ignatius provided records to prove that, if anything, Roser owed the Society. She and Ignatius were later reconciled. Roser became a nun in Barcelona, where she died in 1554. For the most extensive study to date of Ignatius's relationships with Roser and other women, see Rahner, *St. Ignatius of Loyola: Letters to Women.*

2.   Ignatius was memorizing Latin vocabulary, which required him at age thirty-four to sit on benches in a classroom with small boys. Here in *Test.* §55, he juxtaposes the tedium and the seeming irrelevance for his service to others, with the satisfaction that he received from his (supposedly) divine consolations. Later, as superior general, Ignatius had to counsel young Jesuits not to abandon their dry academic studies in favor of a more affectively rewarding ministry. If they obtained theology degrees, church authorities would trust them with positions of influence, and they would possess the intellectual depth to engage people more profoundly. By persevering in studies, they would also grow in the virtues of patience and trust. In short, Jesuits in studies should forego a smaller return now for a greater return later. In 1547, Ignatius expounded these ideas at length in a famous letter to the Jesuits in Coimbra (letter 16, trans. Palmer 165–74). See Ch. 3, no 19.

3.   An excellent example of *agere contra.* See Ch. 3, no 1.

4.   "Although he already had some companions, I think," appears to be Gonçalves's comment that he inserted into the text, to correct Ignatius's assertion that he went to Alcalá alone. Ignatius had recruited four companions in Barcelona (see Ch. 6, nos. 13–16). Ignatius refers to them for the first time in *Test.* §58.

5.   The mockery of saints and prophets was a popular trope in ancient and medieval hagiographies. Closely associated was the idea that God might punish mockers quickly as a warning to others (see 2 Kings 2:23–24). In *Test.* §56, Ignatius perhaps hints at a story that many of his Jesuit readers would have known already. On June 1, 1537, the same day that Ignatius was released from prison in Alcalá (*Test.* §62), a friend named Juan Lucena was asking alms on his behalf from a rich man named Lopez de Mendoza. The latter was angry at Ignatius for having corrected him about his sinful life. Mendoza then scandalized

the people standing around him by saying that if Ignatius was not a hypocrite who deserved to be burned at the stake, then Mendoza himself should be burned alive. That same evening, Mendoza burned to death as the result of a gunpowder accident (*Scripta* 2:136–45).

6.   A wealthy couple, Luís de Antezana and Isabel de Guzman, founded the hospice in 1483 under the name Hospital de Nuestra Señora de la Misericordia. Locals called it the Hospital de Antezana (see Ch. 6, 25). Superintendent Lope Deza took pity on Ignatius and let him stay in the hospice, but it was "out of the frying pan into the fire." Deliberately or not, Deza put him in a wing with a demonic infestation (see Ch. 6, no 9).

7.   Spanish Dominican Domingo de Soto (1494–1560) was a principal figure in the revitalization of Thomistic philosophy in Spain and France. The *Summulae*, a work of logic, was published in 1529; but Ignatius's teachers would have been using earlier manuscript copies. St. Albert the Great (*c.*1193–1280) was a German Dominican, bishop, and teacher of St. Thomas Aquinas; Ignatius studied his *Physicorum libri VIII*, a commentary on Aristotle's natural philosophy. "The Master of the Sentences" was Italian theologian Peter Lombard (*c.*1096–1160), whose four-volume work *The Sentences* was a prerequisite textbook for university students well into the sixteenth century (*Peter Lombard:* The Sentences, trans. Giulio Silano [Toronto: Pontifical Institute of Medieval Studies, 2007–10]). Lombard seems to have inspired various passages that Ignatius wrote in the *Spiritual Exercises* and *Constitutions*, notably the "Principle and Foundation" (*SpirEx.* §23). See *Sentences* book 2, dist. 1, chapter 4, 2:5–6.

8.   "Take the discipline" (*disciplinar* in Spanish). The English words "discipline" and "exercise" are commonly used to translate the ancient Greek word *askēsis*, which was originally a sports term to denote an exercise regimen. Later, the ancient church applied *askēsis* to exercises of a spiritual nature. (Ignatius uses the Spanish word *disciplinas* in this sense in *Test.* §9.) St. Athanasius wrote in the prologue to his *Life of St Antony*: "Since you have asked me about the career of the blessed Antony, hoping to learn how he began the discipline [...] you will want also to emulate his purpose, for Antony's way of life provides monks with a sufficient picture for ascetic practice" (trans. Gregg 29). For the desert fathers and mothers, spiritual exercises

included fasting, keeping vigils, memorizing and pondering scripture verses, and analyzing their thoughts and emotions for anything disordered or influenced by demons. Ignatius's book of *Spiritual Exercises* finds an early inspiration here. Later, in the Middle Ages, "taking the discipline" came to mean, more narrowly, whipping one's own back with a small knotted cord (see Ch. 2, no 3). It was a common means of penance and mortification within Catholic religious orders until the mid-twentieth century. In *Test.* §57, Ignatius seems to imply a demonic restraint on the man's hand.

9.   Comment by Gonçalves in the margins: "I need to recall the fright that [Ignatius] himself got one night" (*FontNarr.* 1:442). Ribadeneira recounted the story in his *Life of Ignatius*: "He once lived at Alcalá in a hospice that they called Antezana [or De misericordia]. At that time that house was well known for its ghosts or nighttime spirits. Ignatius was lodged where they seemed to be the worst. Once, when it was starting to get dark, a shudder ran through his body as he encountered the terrifying look of one of the hostile demons. Immediately he recollected himself. Noticing that the terror was harmless, he fell to his knees. Bursting out with a heartfelt cry, he began to address and challenge the demons. He said, 'If power has been given to you over me by the Lord, I am ready. Use the power you have been given against me; I will not resist or refuse it. But if you have no power, why are you poor, feeble beings raging and terrifying the frightened minds of children with shadowy spirits, and scaring them with empty fright? Or do you want to use false appearances to hurt those that you cannot actually harm?' He said this with such strength of spirit that at that moment he dispelled every fear, and in the future he was much more resolute against all the attacks and terrors of the devil" (trans. Pavur 391–92). For Polanco's account of the same story, see *FontNarr.* 2:545. For precedents, see Ch. 3, no 1, and St. Francis in the *Golden Legend* (trans. Ryan 2:224).

10.   Diego de Eguía (*c.*1488–1556) and his brother Esteban (*c.*1485–1551) were students at the university in Alcalá. They lived in the home of their brother Miguel (1494–1544), a wealthy pioneer of the publishing industry in Spain. Miguel became a benefactor of Ignatius. Miguel published an edition of the *Imitation of Christ* in 1526, during Ignatius's stay in Alcalá de Henares, copies of which still exist. Given Ignatius's

enthusiasm for the book, he possibly asked Miguel to publish it. In 1537, Diego and Esteban reunited with Ignatius in Venice, and they later joined the Society, Diego as a priest (he was already ordained), Esteban as a brother. In 1543, Ignatius made Diego his confessor.

11. "Sack-wearers" (*ensayalados*), from the Spanish *sayal*, meaning coarse wool cloth. In a spirit of poverty, Ignatius and his friends were wearing *sayal*, which inquisitors found problematic for two reasons. First, insofar as the companions wore the same outfit, it looked like a religious habit, which gave people the impression that they were a canonically approved religious group. In the Middle Ages, laypersons often wore the clothing of monks or mendicants, either as a pious gesture, or to convey spiritual authority, or to demonstrate the sincerity of their resolutions to enter a religious congregation. Some even requested burial in religious habits in the hopes of deceiving St. Peter at the Heavenly Gates. Second, the inquisitors were suspicious of Ignatius and his companions because the Illuminati often wore similar clothing (see Ch. 4, no 1 and Ch. 6, no 12).

12. In Ignatius's day, many Spanish Catholics claimed to receive mystical visions and illuminations from God. Today, scholars debate the causes of this phenomenon, and to what extent the mystical experiences were real or imagined. Whatever the truth, many Catholics claimed to have such an intimate relationship with God, and to know his will so perfectly, that they no longer needed the institutional church, with her rituals and moral teachings. Like training wheels on a bicycle, the church was necessary for spiritual beginners, but a hindrance to the more advanced. People called these Catholics *alumbrados* in Spanish, or *Illuminati* in Latin, meaning "enlightened ones." Some inquisitors suspected Ignatius of being an Illuminato because he similarly stressed God's intimate communications with each person. But Ignatius, in accordance with Catholic doctrine, believed that the church is indispensable to every Christian's relationship with God, because it is precisely in the community of faith as such that Jesus had promised to be uniquely present (Matt. 18:20). In the *Spiritual Exercises*, Ignatius urged fidelity to the church, the "true Spouse of Christ our Lord" (§353). His conviction on this matter is key to understanding his decision to obey the Franciscans' order to leave Jerusalem in *Test.* §50. See letter 5205, trans. Palmer 544-549, and Alastair Hamilton, *Heresy and Mysticism in Sixteenth-Century Spain* (Cambridge: James Clarke & Co., 1992).

13. Juan de Arteaga y Avendaño of Estépa (d.1540), from the province of Seville. He joined Ignatius's company in Barcelona in 1524.

14. Calisto de Sa of Segovia. In 1524, Ignatius recommended him as a spiritual director to Inés Pascual (see Ch. 4, no 11), a friend and benefactor in Manresa (letter 1, trans. Palmer 2). Ignatius wrote to her that, "truly, you may discover more in him than appears," which likely alluded to Calisto's tall, lanky frame. People were amused by his enormous hat, and breeches and a cloak that were too short.

15. Lope de Cáceres of Segovia had made the Exercises under Ignatius in Barcelona. Ignatius entrusted him to give spiritual direction to Sr. Rejadell (letter 7, trans. Palmer 1536). Lope, who never followed Ignatius to Paris, should not be confused with Diego de Cáceres, who joined Ignatius in Paris. The latter participated in the so-called "Deliberation of the First Fathers" in Venice in 1539, when Ignatius and his companions elected to begin a new religious order. His name appears in several documents that they drafted at this time (*Const.* 1:8, 13). In 1542, Diego left the Society and became a spy for the French crown. The French eventually suspected him of being a double agent; they tortured him and left him lame (*Chronicon* 1:33, *FontNarr.* 1:170–71, 2:180, 544, 567; *EpistMixtae* 1:72n1).

16. "Little John" (Juanico), i.e., Juan de Reinalde, a seventeen year-old Frenchman who had been wounded in a brawl. Ignatius tended to him while he was recovering, and won him over as a companion. Even before Ignatius left Spain for Paris (*Test.* §71), Juan had departed his company to become a Franciscan in Salamanca. He had probably been frightened by the controversies surrounding Ignatius and sought to join an established order.

17. To receive the Eucharist every eight days was unusually frequent in the early sixteenth century. Many clergy discouraged it for fear that respect for the sacrament would be lost. Here, Ignatius wonders about the benefits of being exonerated by the Inquisition, if priests were still going to refuse him weekly Communion. After the founding of the Society in 1540, the early Jesuits promoted frequent Communion, as did some other religious orders at this time.

18. "Without a fuss [*quietamente*], as in all such matters in which he was ordered." The statement is curious in light of the verbal joust that Ignatius just had with Juan Rodríguez de Figueroa (1490–1565), and

of his other jousts with authorities. It is unlikely that Ignatius was being ironic (see Gonçalves' Foreword, no 7). Perhaps he meant that he had complied with a tranquil confidence in God's providence. Or perhaps he wanted to soften the appearance that he was being disrespectful or disobedient to legitimate authorities. As superior general, Ignatius himself was vexed by various Jesuits who were disobedient or disrespectful, including two of the Society's founding fathers, Simão Rodrigues and Nicolás Bobadilla.

19. Ignatius showed poor judgment by speaking to a married woman alone in his bedroom. He learned from this and many similar mistakes (see *Test.* §97). Later, as superior general, he will emphasize the importance of *caritas discreta*, meaning a charity for others that is regulated by rational prudence (see Kolvenbach, "*Discreta caritas*," *Review of Ignatian Spirituality* 113 [2006]: 9–21, and Geger, "*Cura personalis*," 9–12). The opposite of *caritas discreta* was *zelus non secundum scientiam*, meaning pious enthusiasm that is well intentioned but short-sighted (see Ch. 1, no 19). The latter phrase was inspired by St. Paul's description of his opponents in Romans 10:2; and Ignatius included it in the papal charter of the Society, called the "Formula of the Institute" (trans. Padberg, *Constitutions*, 4–5).

20. Comment by Gonçalves in the margins: "I must remember what Fr. Bustamante told me about this" (*FontNarr.* 1:444). Bartholomé de Bustamante (1501–70) entered the Society in 1552, inspired by the holy example of St. Francis Borgia. He later served as Borgia's secretary. The meaning of Gonçalves's remark is unknown.

21. Comment by Gonçalves in the margins: "M[iona] was one, and was confessor." Fr. Manuel de Miona (*c*.1477–1567) was Ignatius's confessor when the latter was studying in Alcalá, and again later in Paris. He entered the Society in 1545.

22. On March 31, 1492, King Ferdinand and Queen Isabella signed a decree that forced all Jews either to convert to Catholicism or to leave Spain. In the aftermath, Jews were often suspected of having ostensibly converted while continuing to practice their Jewish faith privately on the Sabbath (Saturday). Here, the inquisitors suspect Ignatius of being a secret Jew. According to Polanco, Ignatius responded that the only worship he did on Saturdays was in honor of the Virgin Mary, and that he did not know of other religious practices on Saturdays. He added

that there were no Jews in his country, by which he presumably meant the Basque province of Guipúzcoa (*Chronicon* 1:37, *FontNarr.* 1:170). See James W. Reites, "St. Ignatius of Loyola and the Jews," *Studies in the Spirituality of Jesuits* 13, no. 4 (1981).

23.   "The Veronica" was a term that could denote either the original veil that Veronica used to wipe the face of Jesus or an artistic copy of it. Various cathedrals in Europe claimed to have either the original or a copy, all of which pilgrims came to venerate. In the Cathedral of Jaén in Andalusia is a copy of the veil that probably dates to the fourteenth century.

24.   In the sixteenth century, Spanish culture placed tremendous pressure on women not to travel outside city limits without male escorts. Stable police forces did not exist, while bandits and assailants hid on the road-sides to ambush passersby (*Test.* §87). Moreover, travelers frequently were obliged to walk or ride through the midst of clashing armies, as Ignatius himself experienced (*Test.* §51–53, §72). In *Test.* §61, Ignatius gets into trouble when the Inquisition suspects him of encouraging a mother and daughter to travel without escorts.

25.   "In one hospice or another" (*por unos hospitales y por otros*). In the sixteenth century, the Spanish word *hospital* meant many things. Some were for curing the sick, some were hospices for the dying (*los incurables*), some were poorhouses, while still others were hostels for pilgrims, providing a bed and a meal before they continued on their way. Lexicographer Sebastián de Covarrubias (1539–1613) remarked that, "thanks be to God, there are very few places in all of Spain, for as small as they might be, that do not have a *hospital* for the pilgrims" (*Tesoro* 701, trans. Geger). The absence of modern sanitation and sew-ers meant that many hospitals were extremely unpleasant, but espe-cially those dedicated to people dying of syphilis (see Ch. 8, no 20). In the *Testament*, the word "hospice" is used to translate *hospital*, to better capture the idea that, relative to modern institutions, a greater number of patients did not recover. For lurid descriptions of hospice conditions, see Rodrigues's account in *A Brief and Exact Account: The Recollections of Simão Rodrigues on the Origin and Progress of the Soci-ety of Jesus*, trans. Joseph Conwell (St. Louis, MO: Institute of Jesuit Sources, 2004), 46–48; Georg Schurhammer, *Francis Xavier: His Life, His Times*, 4 vols. (Rome: Jesuit Historical Institute, 1973–82), 1:308, and Jon Arrizabalaga, John Henderson, and Roger French, *The Great*

Pox: The French Disease in Renaissance Europe (New Haven: Yale University Press, 1997), 145–233.

26.   Ignatius did not mean that he knew more theology than the inquisitors, but more than his companions. See *Test.* §64.

27.   See Ch. 4, no 4.

28.   See Ch. 5, no 6.

7. Trouble at Salamanca (July to December 1527)

1.   Comment by Gonçalves in the margins: "And this, of being of the Holy Spirit, is what we would like to find out" (*FontNarr.* 1:454). The question was a trap: if Ignatius answered "from the Holy Spirit," he could be charged with Illuminism. See *Life of St. Antony*, §72–73: "[Antony] was also extremely wise. It was a marvel that although he had not learned letters, he was a shrewd and intelligent man. [Greek philosophers] encountered him in the outer mountain, thinking that they would subject him to ridicule because he had not learned letters. To them Antony said: 'What do you say? Which is first—mind or letters? And which is the cause of which—the mind of the letters, or the letters of the mind?' After their reply that the mind is first, and an inventor of the letters, Antony said: 'Now you see that in the person whose mind is sound there is no need for the letters'" (trans. Gregg 83–84). See also Terence O'Reilly, "The *Spiritual Exercises* and Illuminism in Spain: Dominican Critics of the Early Society of Jesus," in Ite inflammate omnia: *Selected Historical Papers from Conferences Held at Loyola and Rome in 2006*, ed. Thomas M. McCoog (Rome: Institutum Historicum Societatis Iesu, 2010), 199–228.

2.   Desiderius Erasmus (1466–1536), a Dutch priest, was one of the greatest Christian scholars of the sixteenth century. His scathing satires earned many admirers and many critics, the latter believing that he was disrespectful of the church or even heretical. While Ignatius was in Salamanca, some Franciscans and Dominicans were hostile to Erasmus. At the same time that Ignatius was speaking to the Dominicans at San Esteban, a theological conference was being held in Valladolid (June 27 to August 13, 1527), in which twenty-one suspected propositions of Erasmus were examined (Manuel Ruiz Jurado, *Obras de San Ignacio de Loyola* [Madrid: Biblioteca de Autores Cristianos, 1991], 67n2).

3. Gonçalves refers three times to Ignatius's chains (see also *Test.* §69).
    He was alluding to the biblical theme of St. Paul in chains (Acts of the
    Apostles 21:33, 26:29, 28:20, Colossians 4:18, Philippians 1:13–14,
    Ephesians 6:20, Philemon 1:10, 2 Timothy 1:16). The chains that had
    bound the apostle were—and still are—preserved in the basilica of St.
    Paul Outside the Walls, where the first companions made their formal
    profession in the Society of Jesus.

4. Ignatius was speaking to them with the informal *Vos.* See *Test.* §62, and
    Ch. 5, no 6.

5. John 18:23.

6. Acts 26:29

7. Acts of the Apostles 16:25–34. The two companions who remained in
    jail were not Ignatius and Calisto, but Arteaga and Cáceres. The other
    prisoners had discovered that a door was left open. This occurred
    during the three days that Ignatius and Calisto were under house arrest
    in the Dominican monastery (*Test.* §66).

8. The verdict of the Inquisition was not the only reason for Ignatius's move
    to Paris. He faced continuing hostility from many who thought that he
    was an Illuminato, or who mistrusted his close relationships with women.
    Ignatius also believed that his inability to speak French would force him
    to spend more time with his studies, and that in Paris he would be able to
    recruit companions more easily (*Chronicon* 1:40). Years later, his enemies
    in Rome tried to defame him by claiming that his moves to Paris and
    Italy had been flights from imminent prosecution by inquisitors.

9. In the early sixteenth century, both monastic and mendicant religious
    orders were widely perceived—rightly or wrongly—to be guilty of
    laxity and decline. Ignatius's contemporaries St. Teresa of Ávila and
    St. John of the Cross suffered greatly in their attempts to reform their
    Carmelite orders. That being said, the idea of holy persons suffering at
    the hands of lax or misguided religious communities was a recurring
    theme in the desert tradition and medieval hagiographies (see Ch. 1,
    no 26). Thus, Ignatius's references to "decadent" congregations must be
    taken with a grain of salt.

10. "To recruit others with the same resolution, while taking steps to
    keep the companions whom he already had" (*ajuntar algunos del
    mismo propósito, y para conservar los que tenía*). The thematic cou-
    plet of "preservation and increase," expressed in a variety of Spanish

nouns and verbs, appears twelve times in the *Constitutions*, almost all regarding the preservation and increase of the Society in its numbers and spirit (§136, 137, 204, 308, 719, 789, 790, 812–14). It appears hundreds of times in Ignatius's letters, either as part of a formulaic salutation or conclusion, or in the body of the letters; in the latter case, it usually refers to the Society's numbers and spirit (e.g., letters 179, 208, 295, trans. Palmer, 183–88, 211–19, 237–45). Ignatius's immediate inspiration was likely the political philosophy of St. Thomas, specifically his treatise *On Kingship: To the King of Cyprus*, trans. Gerald B. Phelan (Amsterdam: Academische Pers, 1967), which was a primary source for constitutional theory in the sixteenth century (see letter 182, trans. Palmer 195–201). See Ch. 8, no 18.

11. Twice in *Test.* §71, Ignatius affirms that *he* (not *they*) was determined to go to Paris. It is possible that he had insisted on the companions moving to Paris, despite their own reluctance to do so. This would aptly explain why their enthusiasm for their vocations cooled in Ignatius's absence. To his dismay, they never joined him in Paris. A likely reason for their reluctance was the fierce war taking place between Spain and France; in Barcelona, friends tried to stop Ignatius from continuing to Paris, because French soldiers were assaulting Spanish travelers (*Chronicon* 1:41; Ribadeneira, *Life*, book 1:16, trans. Pavur 63).

8. Progress in Paris (February 1528 to April 1535)

1. The words "as he tells me" make it clear that Gonçalves inserted his own commentary directly into the text, as opposed to limiting his observations to the margins of the manuscript. Other passages where the first-person pronoun "I" appears probably should be understood as Gonçalves's remarks (e.g., *Test.* §30, 41, 47, 54, 56).

2. Montaigu was among the strictest of the fifty or more colleges at the University of Paris. Classes began at 5:00 a.m. Both Erasmus and John Calvin (1509–64) had studied there. Later, Ignatius will move to the College of St. Barbara, which represented the meeting point of the old Scholasticism and the new humanism. For a detailed description of student life at the University of Paris, see Philippe Lécrivain, *Paris in the Time of Ignatius of Loyola (1528–1535)*, trans. Ralph C. Renner (St. Louis, MO: Institute of Jesuit Sources, 2011).

3.   Comment by Gonçalves in the margins: "When he was imprisoned in Alcalá, the prince of Spain was born. From this, one can calculate everything, even previous events" (*FontNarr.* 1:464). Philip II (1527–98, r.1556–98) was born in Valladolid on May 21, 1527.

      "The order and method of Paris": Ignatius, now at least thirty-six years old, again sat with small boy in the classroom. But now, he followed a well-planned and organized sequence of studies, which Ignatius later described approvingly in a letter to Fr. Araoz (letter 2226, trans. Palmer 360–63), as opposed to the haphazard procedures in other universities. Later, Ignatius will insist on this "order and method of Paris" for his own schools (*Cons.* §366).

4.   Regents were teachers who lived with students, and who paid them for various tasks. It was also common for students to pay their tuition by working as servants for other students. The young Xavier, at the University of Paris, had another student working for him named Miguel Landívar.

5.   Juan de Castro (1485–1556) was born in Burgos in 1485, and received his doctorate in theology in October 1532. He came from a noble family, and was a prestigious student at the University of Paris. His family and friends expected an illustrious career from him, for which reason they became angry when Castro chose to imitate Ignatius's example of poverty and service to others (*Test.* §77).

6.   Pedro de Peralta, from the diocese of Toledo, was a distinguished student working toward a master's degree in theology. In 1532, inspired by Ignatius, he attempted to make a pilgrimage to Jerusalem, but his own family had him apprehended when he was passing through Italy. In 1534, he became canon of the cathedral in Toledo, where he remained until at least 1554. Nothing is known of his later life.

7.   Amador de Elduayén was from a noble family in the Basque province of Guipúzcoa, in the diocese of Pamplona. He was not as academically distinguished as Castro and Peralta, but he was the first of the three to make the Spiritual Exercises under Ignatius.

8.   Castro earned his doctorate in theology on October 25, 1532, and entered the Carthusian monastery of Vall de Cristo in Segorbe, Valencia, on June 23, 1535. He became prior of the monastery of Porta Coeli near Valencia in 1542, where he died on July 6, 1556, a few weeks before Ignatius's own death. Here in *Test.* §78, Ignatius incorrectly calls

a Carthusian monk a "friar" (*fraile*, *FontNarr.* 1:468). Friars properly so-called are members of mendicant orders (e.g., Franciscans, Dominicans, Augustinians, Carmelites); they differ from monks insofar as they leave their residences to serve others in spiritual and corporal works of mercy.

9.   That Ignatius attempted to recruit a man who essentially had stolen his money suggests that he was not yet sufficiently discriminating. This would haunt him later when he accepted into his group two dubious characters named Miguel Landívar (*Test.* §98) and Antonio Arias. See Barton T. Geger, "The *First* First Companions: The Continuing Impact of the Men Who Left Ignatius," *Studies in the Spirituality of Jesuits* 44, no. 2 (Summer 2012): 16–21.

     "Under those circumstances" refers to the fact that Ignatius was taking advantage of the man's potentially fatal illness to get him thinking about his mortality and the things of God. Ignatius surely would have been thinking of his own conversion experience (see Ch. 1, no. 11). Similarly, he converted "Little John" while the latter was recovering from being injured in a brawl.

10. Christians commit the sin of "tempting God" when they try to force God's hand in some manner, e.g., when parents expect God to work a miracle for their sick child instead of taking them to the hospital, or when a person says to God, "If you really love me, then you will do this for me, otherwise I will cease to believe in you." Tempting God should not be confused with the legitimate Catholic practice of prayers and fasting undertaken for the sake of winning graces for oneself and others (*SpirEx.* §87), since the granting of these are either left to God's freedom, or—in the case of indulgences, for example—they are promised by the church in her rightful capacity as distributor of the superabundance of graces won by Christ and the saints. That being said, the line between trusting God and tempting God is often blurry, thus Ignatius's dilemma whether he should cross the Mediterranean with or without money (*Test.* §35–36).

11. In SpirEx. §41, Ignatius wrote that "one should say nothing to defame another or to spread gossip, because if I make known a mortal sin which is not public knowledge, I sin mortally, and if the sin is venial, I sin venially, while if it is a defect, I show my own defect." Ignatius added that exceptions were possible in two cases only: (1) if the sins

are already public knowledge and are corrupting the minds of others, or (2) if one reasonably expects to help other people spiritually by relating the sins to them. Thus, the fact that Ignatius records for posterity the sins and defects of these men indicates that he believed that one or both considerations were in play. With regard to Arteaga, Ignatius certainly did not consider episcopal ordination sinful in itself. At that time, however, men often sought the office for its riches, honors, and privileges. Hence, a number of reputable nominees refused the seat in Chiapas, Mexico, before Arteaga finally accepted it (see Marcel Bataillon, "L'iñiguiste et la beata: Premier voyage de Calisto à México," *Revista de historia de América* 31 [1951]: 59–75). In that historical context, many Catholics would have perceived Arteaga, rightly or wrongly, as having fallen from the ideals of Ignatius.

12. Doña Leonor de Mascarenhas (1503–84) was born into a high-ranking noble family in Portugal. In 1526, she went to Spain as companion to Infanta Isabella (1503–39); the latter married Emperor Charles V, thus becoming Holy Roman empress and queen of Spain. Leonor was strongly devout: when she was a teenager, she elected to be celibate, and in the Spanish court, she wore a Franciscan habit and used her political resources to care for the poor. In 1527, Isabella made Leonor the governess of her first child, Prince Philip. Ignatius met Leonor that same year. She remained a benefactor and protector of the Society her entire life. See Rahner, *Letters to Women*, 417–33.

13. When Calisto failed to arrive in Paris, he deeply embarrassed both Ignatius and Doña Leonor, both of who had vouched for him to the king of Portugal. Instead, Calisto went to Mexico City with a *beata* named Catalina Hernández to establish a school for native girls. His relationship with her caused scandal, and he was expelled from the city. He became wealthy in the Americas, and then returned to live in Salamanca, where only a few years before, he had been serving the poor alongside Ignatius. His lavish lifestyle, and the fact that he had abandoned his vocation with Ignatius, scandalized the Salamancans. One can guess Ignatius's reaction when he heard the news.

14. On the significance of the word "resolution" (*propósito*), see Ch. 1, no. 24. In the First Letter to Timothy 5:3–16, the sacred writer rebukes Christian widows who chose to remarry, after they had made a public declaration to their community that they would dedicate the rest of

their lives to the service of the church as single women. In verse 12, the writer notes that they broke their "first pledge," which St. Jerome translated into Latin as "first faith" (*primam fidem*) in the Vulgate Bible. Hence, in the ancient and medieval church, "to break one's first resolution" or "to break one's first faith" came to mean a betrayal of a solemn religious commitment.

15. A *comendador* was a commander in a military order of knights—such as the Order of Santiago, founded in the twelfth century to protect pilgrims on the Camino—who received certain benefits, income, or rewards by virtue of that office. Military orders followed a religious rule—in the case of the Order of Santiago, for example, the Rule of St. Augustine—and they received ecclesial recognition as monastic religious orders.

16. Arteaga died on September 8, 1540. His successor was the saintly Bartolomé de las Casas (*c.*1484–1566). Water of Soliman was a clear antiseptic.

17. French Dominican Matthieu Ory (1482–1557). Both he and Figueroa were in Rome at the same time that Ignatius and his companions were suffering the most severe of the persecutions against them (see Ch. 11, no. 2). Their testimony was crucial to the companions' exoneration.

18. "Retaining those companions who had the same resolution to serve the Lord, but not to go in search of others" (*el entrò con proposito de conservar quelli, che havevano proposto di servir' al Signore; ma non andare più inanzi a cercar'altro*). A medieval axiom, inspired by the Roman poet Ovid in *Ars Amatoriae* 2:13, held that "it is no less a virtue to preserve what one has created than to have created it in the first place" (*Non minor est virtus quam querere, parta tueri*). As superior general, Ignatius cited this axiom to Polanco when discussing the importance of the Society taking steps to ensure that its men persevered in their vocations (*Polanco* 2:734–35). See Ch. 7, no. 10.

19. Peter Faber (*Pierre Favre* in French) was a pious farm boy from Savoy, and the first companion of Ignatius to persevere. Francis Xavier (*Francisco Javier* in Spanish) was a wealthy nobleman from Navarre whose family was on the French side in the battle at Pamplona. As they were Ignatius's first permanent recruits, it is surprising that he does not say more about them here. Ignatius recruited numerous men during his studies in Paris, some of whom persevered with him to found the Society, and some who did not (see Ch. 8, no. 22).

20.   In an age when modern sanitation did not exist, Christians who cared
       for the sick and dying in hospices were often tempted to quit from the
       stench of feces, vomit, body odors, and festering sores, and from fear of
       contagion (see Ch. 6, no. 25). To do something deliberately repugnant
       in order to defeat that temptation was a classic tactic of the spiritual
       life, and an excellent example of the broader principle of *agere contra*
       (see Ch. 3, no. 1). Kissing lepers was a common gesture in medieval
       literature. In the *Golden Legend*, St. Francis kissed a leper to overcome
       his disgust (Ryan 2:221). St. Catherine of Siena pressed her lips to an
       infected wound (Lamb, *Life of St. Catherine of Siena*, 141). In 1537,
       when Xavier was caring for victims of syphilis in Venice, he put his
       hand in his mouth (*Chronicon* 1:57).

21.   The meaning of "to take a stone" (*tomar una piedra*) has long eluded
       scholars. It seems to mean a custom of students sitting on a stone
       when taking final exams for the bachelor's degree (see Jurado, *Obras*,
       82n24; *FontNarr.* 1:478n20). The 1570 statutes for taking the bach-
       elor's exams at the University of St. Andrews, Scotland, likewise
       describes students taking exams while sitting *super lapidem*. It
       suggests that all students were required to take a stone to obtain a
       degree, as Ignatius himself seems to imply in *Test.* §84. In that case,
       his choice would have been to pay money for the degree, or, in a spirit
       of poverty, to continue studies without the degree. However, Rib-
       adeneira asserted that the stone was an optional, harder exam that
       students could take in order to demonstrate their academic prowess
       (book 2, chapter 1, trans. Pavur 68). In that case, Ignatius would have
       been concerned that taking the stone would look like he was spend-
       ing money on a vanity project. Either way, Ignatius and Master Peña
       must have concluded that taking the stone would give him greater
       credibility among church authorities.

22.   Earlier in the *Testament*, Ignatius referred many times to various
       "companions," but here, his reference to *the* companions (*li compagni*)
       refers more narrowly to six men who finally persevered with him and
       who helped him to found the Society: Faber, Xavier, Laínez, Salmerón,
       Bobadilla, and Rodrigues. *Test.* §85 makes this clear. (In subsequent
       endnotes, these will be called "Companions" with a capital C.) In 1534,
       Ignatius gave the Spiritual Exercises to all of them: to Faber in January,
       to Laínez and Salmerón in spring, to Rodrigues and Bobadilla a little

later, and to Xavier in September, after he had taken the vow along with the others at Montmartre on August 15.

23. Ignatius seems to imply that all the Companions were in agreement about spending the rest of their lives in Jerusalem, provided that they could get there. In fact, they were divided. Ignatius, Xavier, and Laínez favored staying, while Faber and Rodrigues wanted to return. They decided to wait until they had spent several months in Jerusalem, after which they all would abide by the majority vote (Schurhammer, *Francis Xavier*, 1:210–12).

24. Later in the *Testament*, Ignatius neglects to recount the day when the Companions made their formal offering to the pope. Likewise, most of the other first Jesuits were oddly silent about this momentous event in their own memoirs and letters. However, on November 22, 1538, Faber did indicate in a letter to Dr. Diego de Gouveia (*c.*1471–1557) that they had met with the pope, at which time they had "signified to him that we are ready for whatever he may decide for us in Christ" (letter 16, trans. Palmer 33). In his memoirs, Faber described that same day: "That same year [of 1538], after the verdict that cleared us, we were favored with a very special grace which is, as it were, the foundation stone of our whole Society [*quasi totius Societatis fundamentum*]. We offered ourselves as a holocaust to the sovereign pontiff Paul III so that he himself could determine what way we might be able to serve Christ and do good to all those who are under authority to the Apostolic See, while we ourselves led a life of perpetual poverty, holding ourselves ready to set off at his order for the uttermost point of the Indies. The Lord willed that he should receive us and show himself pleased with what we proposed" (*FontNarr.* 1:42; trans. Murphy 72). Faber's description of that day as the Society's "foundation" suggests that this is what Ignatius had in mind when he referred to "the earliest foundation" (*primera institución*) of the Society in the opening line of the General Examen in the Jesuit *Constitutions* (*Cons.* §1). Bobadilla also refers to that day in a letter of July 1539 (*Bobadilla* 16).

25. Ignatius had more reasons to return to Spain than his health. He wished to make amends to the people of Azpeitia for the poor example he had set in his youth, and he wished to visit the parents of his Companions to assure them that their sons were safe and well. A popular myth holds that Ignatius returned to Azpeitia also to make

provisions for an illegitimate daughter. In 1988, a document was discovered in which the daughter of Don Antonio Manrique de Lara,
the duke whom Ignatius served for three years, mentioned a María
Villarreal de Loyola. It launched speculation that Ignatius was María's
father. The *New York Times* even ran a story on August 24, 1991. There
is no direct evidence to support that theory. Circumstantial evidence
suggests that María was the child of Pedro de Villarreal from Pedroso.
Given the massive fund of documents that exists about every aspect
of Ignatius's life, produced by hundreds of people who knew him
personally, and given Ignatius's many enemies who would have been
only too happy to accuse him of neglecting an illegitimate child, it
seems hardly possible that no one would have mentioned a daughter.
See José Martínez de Toda, "María Villareal de Loyola, ¿presunta hija
de Íñigo de Loyola?"; *Archivum Historicum Societatis Iesu* 75 (2006),
325–60. See also Fr. Araoz's extended comments on Ignatius's reasons for returning to Azpeitia (*Scripta* 1: 727–30).

26. See also *Test.* §98. On several occasions, inquisitors received complaints
about Ignatius, after which they told him that they would not conduct
an investigation, because they already believed that he was innocent.
To their surprise, Ignatius insisted that they investigate him anyway. It
was not enough for him that God and the inquisitors knew him to be
innocent. The accusations had damaged his reputation, so that Catholics were wary of seeking his help. They too needed to know his inno-
cence. The inquisitors conceded reluctantly, because the investigations
cost much time and paperwork. Here is just one practical implication
of Ignatius's commitment to the greater glory of God. Had his primary
interest been his personal sanctification, he might have embraced slan-
ders as opportunities for penance and humility, as indeed many saints
would have recommended.

9. Farewell to Spain (October to November 1535)

1. The province of Guipúzcoa, in which Azpeitia is located.
2. The idea that persons committed to following Christ should distance themselves from their families was a staple of medieval spiritualities. Ludolph wrote in the *Life of Christ*: "Those who want to cling to God should not dwell with their family members, but rather should distance themselves from them. [...] Bernard says, 'O good Jesus, if you were not found among your own relatives, how can I expect to find you among mine?'" (trans. Walsh 1:308–9).
3. As lord of Loyola Castle, Martín Loyola was embarrassed at the prospect of his brother being shabbily dressed in public, evangelizing Martín's friends and associates, and teaching children. Thus in §87, he insisted that Ignatius stay at the castle. In the *Golden Legend*, Francis's shabby clothing embarrasses his wealthy family (Ryan 2:220). When the Society of Jesus was founded, all the Companions except Bobadilla agreed that they should require professed Jesuits to teach catechism to children once a year, partly in order to preserve their own humility. See Conwell, *Impelling Spirit*, 176–81.
4. Three Carthusians named Anthony Martin, Andrew Soler, and Nicholas Bonet, later attested that during Ignatius's stay with them in 1535, he described to the monks his vision for the new religious institute that he was planning to establish. Upon hearing this, Castro offered to re-join Ignatius. The pilgrim refused, telling Castro that he should honor his commitment to the Carthusians (Daniello Bartoli, *History of the Life and Institute of St. Ignatius de Loyola, Founder of the Society of Jesus* [New York: E. Dunigan, 1855], 2:245–46). The sources that Fr. Bartoli [1608–85] cites do not appear to be in the MHSI). Ignatius did not want to give the appearance of scalping vocations from a friendly religious order, a concern that he reiterated frequently as superior general (*Cons.* §171; *Epist.* 2:386, 722, 3:136, 7:291, 712, 8:41, 673, 9:384–85, 10:119, 12:229–30, 676; *Laínez* 2:683–85). Such tensions were common in the history of Catholic religious life.

    Ignatius also would have doubted anyone willing to abandon his *propósito* not once but twice (see Ch. 1, no. 24). In the *Constitutions*, he wrote that a man should not be accepted into the Society if he has "taken the habit of a religious institute of friars or clerics, by living under obedience with them for a time, whether profession was made or not; or the case of having been a hermit in monastic garb" (§27), the reason being that "it appears to us in our Lord that every good Christian ought to be stable in his first vocation [*primera vocación*], above all when it is so holy, one in which he has abandoned all the world and dedicated himself completely to the greater service and glory of his Creator and Lord" (§30). On the expression "first vocation," see Ch. 8, no. 14.

10. Venice and Vicenza (January 1536 to October 1537)

1. There is no diocese of Cette. Gonçalves's scribe probably meant to write *Chieti*, whose bishop Gian Pietro Carafa (1476–1559) was the Theatine cardinal mentioned in *Test.* §93, and later Pope Paul IV.

2. While Ignatius was in Spain, his six Companions at the University of Paris managed to recruit three more: Paschase Broët (*c.*1500–62), Codure, and Claude Le Jay (*c.*1500–52). See John W. Padberg, "The Three Forgotten Founders of the Society of Jesus: Paschase Broët, Jean Codure, Claude Jay," *Studies in the Spirituality of Jesuits* 29, no. 2 (March 1997).

3. The Companions were Spanish, French, and Portuguese. As their countries were at war with each other, the men took a simple step to promote closer bonds between them. After the foundation of the Society in 1540, its emphasis on apostolic mobility meant that Jesuits often were required to walk through territories or encampments that were at war with their own countries (e.g., Eaglestone §163). Moreover, relative to other religious orders, Jesuit communities were more international in composition, so that Jesuits often found themselves sitting across the dinner table from men from hostile countries. For these reasons among others, Ignatius made a "union of minds and hearts" between Jesuits (*unión de los ánimos*) the subject of an entire chapter in the *Constitutions* (chapter 8, §655–718).

4. Ignatius was ordained a priest on June 24, 1537. As he still fervently desired to spend the rest of his life in Jerusalem, he waited a whole year to celebrate his first Mass, hoping that he could do so there. When it became clear to the Companions that the Third Ottoman–Venetian War (1537–40) would prevent them from sailing to the Holy City, Ignatius celebrated his first Mass on Christmas Day, 1538. He chose a location closest in spirit to Jerusalem: the basilica of St. Mary Major in Rome, in a side-chapel dedicated to the infant Jesus in the manger (*FontNarr.* 1:36).

5. *Ad titulum paupertatis* (under the title of poverty). In the sixteenth century, the church was vexed with the problem of thousands of illiterate and/or unemployed priests with little or no means of sustenance. Consequently, church law required that candidates for ordination identify the means of their future support. For diocesan clergy, this could be a parish where they had been assured a position, or a benefice, or a family inheritance. Members of religious orders could be ordained "under the title of poverty," meaning that they would be sustained by their own communities and their benefactors. But since Ignatius and his Companions were not yet a formal religious order, they needed a dispensation to use that title (*FontDoc.* 532). In a letter to Juan Verdolay, Ignatius indicated that they also had the option to be ordained *ad titulum sufficientis litteraturae* (under the title of sufficient learning), meaning that they could sustain themselves by teaching if they so chose (letter 12, trans. Palmer 29). The Companions chose to accept both titles, of poverty and of sufficient learning. See Conwell, *Impelling Spirit*, 76–78.

6. Gonçalves uses the word *sopranaturali* (supernatural) as a quasi-technical term to indicate that Ignatius's mystical experiences were an extraordinary, spontaneous gift from God that Ignatius could not have generated by means of his own powers of concentration and will. St. Teresa frequently referred to the *sobrenatural* in prayer: "The first prayer I experienced that in my opinion was supernatural (a term I use for what cannot be acquired by effort or diligence, however much one tries, although one can dispose oneself for it which would help a great deal) is an interior recollection felt in the soul" (*Spiritual Testimonies* 5.3; trans. Kavanaugh 1:425).

7. Ignatius refers to Rodrigues. For the latter's account, see Conwell, *Brief and Exact*, 62–63.

8. In the *Golden Legend*, St. Dominic is in Rome seeking papal permission to found a new order, when he receives a mystical vision, in which Mary presents both him and St. Francis to Jesus (Ryan 2:47–48).

9. Comment by Gonçalves in the margins: "And I who am writing these things, said to the pilgrim, when he told me this, that Laínez recounted it with other details—so I understood. He told me that everything that Laínez said was true, because he did not recall it in such detail, but that at the moment when he narrated it, he was certain that he had said nothing but the truth. He said the same to me about other things"

(*FontNarr.* 1:498). The best study of the early sources regarding this vision continues to be Hugo Rahner, *The Vision of St. Ignatius in the Chapel of La Storta, Second Edition* (Rome, 1979).

11. Finally in Rome (November 1537 to October 1538)

1. The priest Diego de Hoces (*c*.1490–1538) was a native of Málaga. At first, he was suspicious of Ignatius, but he made the Exercises and became Ignatius's follower. He died in Padua on or about March 13. Traditionally, Jesuits call Hoces the first to die in the Society, even though the Society did not yet formally exist. In the desert and medieval traditions, Christians often reported seeing other Christians enter heaven (e.g., *Life of St. Antony* §60, 66, Ward, *Sayings of the Desert Fathers*, 94; *The Golden Legend* regarding Saints Dominic and Francis [Ryan 2:54–55, 228–29], St. Teresa, *Book of Her Life* 38, trans. Kavanaugh 1:329–42).

2. Miguel Landívar was a student at the University of Paris who paid his tuition by working as a servant for Xavier. He lost his job when Francis chose to imitate Ignatius's example of poverty. He was emotionally unstable and easily manipulated, and Ignatius later erred grievously by letting him join the Companions. Landívar and another recruit named Antonio Arias stood with the Companions when they asked Pope Paul III for permission to be ordained and to make a pilgrimage to the Holy Land. Only a few days later, they defected, and then publicly accused the Companions of heresy and "immoral behavior," a euphemism for sexual misconduct. The Inquisition investigated and exonerated the Companions, but the public uproar lasted eight months, and seriously threatened papal approbation of the nascent Society. Ignatius wrote a detailed account in a letter to Roser (letter 18, trans. Palmer, *Ignatius of Loyola*, 35–39). See Geger, "*First* First Companions," 16–21.

3. This letter is probably the one that is critically edited in *EpistMixae* 1:11–14.

4. See Ch. 8, no. 26.

5. Ignatius recounted his visit to the pope in a letter to Roser (letter 18, trans. Palmer, 35–39).

6. The abrupt ending is significant. Ignatius and/or Gonçalves expected Nadal—and probably other Jesuits as well—to assist in the completion of *A Pilgrim's Testament*.

Epilogue of Fr. Gonçalves

1. *SpirEx.* §31.
2. *SpirEx.* §169–89.
3. Ignatius had been convinced of his duty to dictate his memoirs, because he believed it would serve God's greater glory (see Gonçalves' Foreword no. 3). Nevertheless, after he was finished, he still worried that he would be perceived as vain. It is a helpful reminder that saints are still human beings. On "pure intention," see Ch. 2, no. 8.
4. Gonçalves refers to the so-called "Spiritual Diary," which was not really a diary per se, but rather a notebook in which Ignatius recorded his experiences of prayer and discernment. Apparently, most of those notes have been lost—the "rather large bundle" mentioned by Gonçalves— but the surviving remnants extend from February 2, 1544 to February 27, 1545 (trans. Munitiz and Endean, *Saint Ignatius of Loyola*, 70–109). There, Ignatius recorded his efforts to discern God's will regarding a point of vowed poverty for Jesuit churches. He listed both the rational pros and cons of each option, and his consolations and desolations when praying over the matter (see Ch. 1, no. 15).
5. The *Testament* refers repeatedly to Ignatius's tears (§18, 28, 33, 98, 100, 101). In the desert tradition, copious tears of compunction or consolation were a reliable indicator of progress in spiritual perfection (e.g., Ward, *Desert Fathers*, 12–18; Cassian, *Conferences* 9:27–30, trans. Ramsey 346–49). In medieval spirituality, a supernatural "gift of tears" was closely associated with mystical contemplation. The gift is attributed to numerous saints in the *Golden Legend*, including Peter, Paul, and Mary Magdalene (trans. Ryan 1:340, 358, 375). See the prologue to the *Life of Christ* (trans. Walsh 1:5), *Imitation of Christ* 2:21, 55, 4:11; *Snares of the Devil* 3:2. Faber referred often to his tears in his spiritual diary, even expressing surprise at their absence (trans. Murphy 126). St. Teresa noted that God gave her the gift of tears at an early age (*Book of Her Life* 4:7; trans. Kavanaugh 1:67), and she linked it to her spiritual progress (9:1, 7–8; trans. Kavanaugh 1:101, 103).

    Ignatius wept so frequently during Mass and the Divine Office that it endangered his eyesight. His doctors ordered him not to weep, and the pope gave him a dispensation from praying the office (Eaglestone §183, 301, *Scripta* 1:552–53, *FontNarr.* 2:158). In the *Golden Legend*, St. Francis's eyesight is also impaired by his weeping, and his friends urge him to stop (Ryan 2:226). In 1553, Polanco wrote a letter on behalf of Ignatius to a Jesuit who desired the gift of tears, warning him that it can exhaust people mentally and physically, and thereby make them less available for service to others (letter 3924, trans. Palmer 449–50). See Martin, Maurice-Marie. "The Mysticism of St. Ignatius: The Gift of Tears in the Spiritual Diary." *The Spiritual Diary of St. Ignatius: Linguistic Analysis and Mystical Theology*. Vol. 22.2, no. 67. Rome, Centrum Ignatianum Spiritualitatis, 1991, and Kimberly Patton and John Hawley, eds., *Holy Tears: Weeping in the Religious Imagination* (Princeton: Princeton University Press, 2005).

Index